LORD OF
GARBAGE

VOLUME ONE

BY

KIM FOWLEY

KICKS BOOKS

NEW YORK, NEW YORK

NOTE FROM THE PUBLISHER

Kim Fowley is the last standing knight from the original Cool World roundtable. He prefers to think of himself as the Lord Of Garbage. This mind mangling collage of his poetry and prose provides a wild ride into the early years of a musical mastermind and juvenile delinquent, as he drives deep into the dark recesses of a life fraught with pain, fame, and mayhem. You already know the genius music. Now, know the genius man of letters.

Thank you, Kim Fowley.

LORD OF GARBAGE (VOLUME ONE)

Copyright © 2012 by Kicks Books

Published in 2012 by Kicks Books
PO Box 646 Cooper Station
New York NY 10276

Printed in the United States of America

ISBN: 978-09659777-6-0

Editor: Miriam Linna
Editorial Assistance: Gigi Himmel
Design: Patrick Broderick/Rotodesign

www.kicksbooks.com

IN MEMORIAM

ALAN FREED
who understood my need
to learn and be great

&

GENE VINCENT
who showed me that being crippled
was a plus and not a minus

the lord of garbage
is an unloved
unwanted child
born torn
and shopworn
from embryo
to crypt
from bassinette
to bath tub
let's hide this
battered baby
monster child
from normalcy
and decency
from help and happiness
let's pretend
KVF
does not exist

DEDICATIONS
ACKNOWLEDGEMENTS
KIM FOWLEY

Rock and roll is driven by revenge and sex. The revenge part is directed against mean family members, unfriendly friends, resentful school teachers, and neighborhood enemies who always thought you were a loser with no talent, no magic, no future.

The sex part is all the boys and girls that your future rock and roll hero wanted to love that didn't know you were in the same room with them.

They didn't even know you were alive.

It was these missing links who drove me to the top of the charts time and time again. The revenge people never did acknowledge my vinyl victories.

(1939-1969) I did the whole ladder of success climb alone.

No one was ever there. No one ever cared.

LORD OF GARBAGE is dedicated to the members of the biz, media and audience who consumed my jukebox jungle creations during the first thirty years of my life.

LORD OF GARBAGE is also dedicated to Sarah, Snow and Little Sex Fat, who forty-two years before this book ends, turned up in my terrible life to hold me tight on these dark, dangerous nights. Thank you, ladies.

Enjoy LORD OF GARBAGE. It will tell you why I was born to make you cry.

www.kimfowley.com

the lord of garbage
is a magic kid
mini monster
to a movie colony
look out for cops
while the old man shovels
drugs down his body
he lives to drink
not great
almost talented
he and the garbage man's mother
aren't good enough to be great
don't they know
I am a future god?

INTRODUCTION

BY KIM FOWLEY

THIS IS A WARNING. Not an intro to a book. *Lord of Garbage* is the raving of a rock n' roll madman.

I wrote the prose part of the book during bladder cancer recall surgery hospital stays. My diet included morphine, IV drips, and bladder bags. No wife. No child. No friends. Just blood and thunder, puke, piss, scabs, and teardrops.

Death is my next long term project. But before I slide, glide, or crawl out of this black and white guts splattered life, I wanted to get my story down on slabs of parchment. So you folks know that a monster crept among you, through the vinyl jungle and cinema graveyard of a dark and dangerous trance. Yes, I grunted out enough bile for a three volume set.

Lord of Garbage is the first blood book in a three volume sicko series. Kicks Books chose to do it in these necessary installments, because there's no way that you could have digested all of this wicked waste in one long vacuum gulp.

Everything is done. Turned in. Finished.

FYI, the poems were all written at the time that the prose happened. This indicates that I was ahead of my time. The Outlaw King of America is not only a King of the Creeps—I am the Wizard of Words. I am the King of Slime.

Read *Lord of Garbage* at your own peril. You are taking a risk. Enjoy this SOS FROM HELL!

Kim Fowley
Autumn 2012
West Hollywood, California

lord of garbage
breathes gasoline and teardrops
reads hate mail in the world's eyes
hears about himself on the grapevine
that runs from his broken heart

lord of garbage
is not easy to know
can't smile because of early childhood rotten
teeth
too tall, too thin,
keeps it all within
a wisp of a giant
giraffe and elk
tower of terror
tearing down clouds
from a frightened sky

lords of garbage
throughout the ages
scream from pages
of parchment white
spending nights alone
fighting snipers and vipers
deep in the combat zone
        "garbage man!" she yelled
        and garbage girls screamed

we want to drink the juice
from the lion's paws

lord of garbage
knows you will not approve
of my need to nosh in greasy spoons
the lord of garbage
needs a wild witch
hummingbirds in velvet
jesus chocolate pie
and paper rose

lord of garbage
needs a steady hand of sweet relief
to rescue the ostrich girl from
the clutches of the indian chief

the lord of garbage
has energy drainers in every time zone
waiting to clip the wings of a visionary
bent in half by censorship and restriction
hail hail rock and roll!
who gave the enemy full control
no one alive has heard as much as me
I can't blend in but I haven't lost the energy
your lordship in on the edge of eternity

my funeral will not be well attended
I will be laid to rest in an even row
of sandstone tombstones
an unmarked grave will be my fate
but if an inscription does exist
it will read:
>born too late to make a difference
>born too late to make a change

lord of garbage
finds you weeping
everyone was afraid
he was so evil
he was so strange
future lords of garbage
make believe you are a saint
disguise and hide yourself
don't be tempted or you'll be sorry
if you're caught ...
>in pagan paint

LORD OF GARBAGE

When you think of Kim Fowley, think of a child born in the black and white world of 1939. Between 1939 and 1957, I took in eighteen years of a Dickens-type childhood. Dysfunctional parents, of course. Isn't that the way it should be? There has to be something wrong in order to be driven mad. I've always been a genius. I'm also an idiot savant, with physical handicaps. I got polio, otherwise known as permanent paralysis, in 1944. It was more horrifying than it should have been. I'd been pawned off into a foster home three years earlier, as a two-year-old. That was how life started for me in California, USA.

July 21, 1939. That was the day that Hitler invaded Poland. Well, maybe he didn't. But he might have. Regardless, and more importantly, KIM FOWLEY—Kim Vincent Fowley—*did* show up, kicking and screaming, ejected at precisely 9:46 PM from the loins of debutante-*cum*-starlet Shelby Payne, at St. Vincent's Hospital in Los Angeles. Shelby's first child. Doug Fowley's first son. Shelby Payne was Dorothy Lamour meets Natalie Wood—selfish, vain, bright but not brilliant, brooding—a spoiled bitch from Oregon, the Beaver State. Her father was William Wallace Payne, the lumber tycoon. He died mysteriously in 1932 after the stock market crashed. As for my father, Daniel Vincent "Douglas" Fowley grew up in New York City, born in the Bronx to Irish immigrant milkman/sculptor/motorcycle rider John Fowley and his wife Anna.

So, a child was born and started life on Wetherly Drive, between Burton Way and Wilshire Boulevard, in beautiful Beverly Hills, with a bad boy dad and silver spoon mother. Dad was more interested in me than Mom was. She wanted her little monster in diapers to grow up fast, so she could dress me up as a leading man and haul me around Hollywood. My father, on the other hand, didn't want to show me off, because I'd be competition for him. He was afraid of competition.

We went from Wetherly Drive in Beverly Hills to Tigertail Road in Brentwood, another rich, white part of town. Tigertail Road was upscale, much more so than Wetherly Drive, which is in a boring part of Beverly Hills. There's no poor part of Beverly Hills, but there *are* boring parts.

Kim Fowley could talk at ten months, could read and write by one and a half. It freaked out my mom, so she placed me in a foster home. The problem started for me and my mother around 1940, maybe. It was just before my first birthday, and all her family members were there, waiting for baby's first word. I was the baby. Only my first words weren't "Mama" or "Dada."

My first words were, "I have a question. Why are you bigger than me?" What they should have done was pick me up off the floor, put me in a high chair and say, "Welcome to conversational adult America. When did you learn how to form sentences? How brilliant are you? You're a gifted child and we'd love to know more about you."

Instead my mother picked me up, started crying, and pushed me away from her like I was a stinking piece of meat, then grabbed me under her arm and ran across the lawn into the dressing room near the swimming pool. She put me on the floor.

"I gave birth to a fucking genius," was her statement. And she turned on the record player. There was a Carmen Miranda record on it. I couldn't read then, but I recognized the music and there was a picture of the RCA dog on this shellac 78, a real heavy thing.

"Okay, little baby," she said. "Enjoy the music." So she slammed the door, and ran back to the house and everyone consoled her because she had a little baby who spoke in complete sentences.

I learned two things that day, dear reader. One, be careful what you say to insensitive people. And two, welcome to the music business. Oh, they're going to park me in music and I'm supposed to interact with a spinning disc? Is that what my reality's gonna be? So be it. I'd better get used to this, because I don't want to be beat up. I don't want to be murdered. I don't want to be hurt. So I will try to watch my tongue, to watch what I say.

Another year goes by. I had a dog named Rusty, an Irish setter. One day the Japanese planes bombed Pearl Harbor. My dad ran off and joined the US Navy to kick ass. Dad's gone. Mom donates Rusty to the Canine Corps, and decides to dump me off on her mother in Portland, Oregon. She is hoping that Dad will die in battle and that she can marry husband number two, a rich guy, because my dad was just a B-movie actor. She needed a rich guy.

I remember going from L.A. to Portland in 1941, during the blackouts. They thought the Japanese were going to come over in their airplanes and bomb the West Coast of America, so there were blackouts and air wardens and the train had no lights, and the windows had black curtains. When we got to Portland, we went to Mom's ancestral home on Aspen Street.

I had my own room. My mother parked me there and went back to Hollywood. She was an aspiring actress at that point, and like all women during wartime, she was also Rosie the Riveter, making airplanes. There was no gasoline, and there was no hosiery. They were making war materials out of oil products and whatever makes up nylons.

So little Kim Fowley got to sit up in Portland and wait for Mommy. One day my grandmother took me to see *Bambi*. I knew something was wrong, because I had never been taken to a movie theatre before. I was allowed to listen to the radio. I heard *Our Girl Sunday* and Lux Radio Theatre and Lowell Thomas. The Dorsey Brothers had some sort of show, and I heard a lot of Ferde Grofé doing *Grand Canyon Suite* and stuff like *Rhapsody In Blue*.

After *Bambi*, she took me to the dentist and the dentist said, "This boy is going to have a lifetime of dental problems. He has an upside down bite, a deformity." My grandmother calls my mother, crying, "He's deformed! I don't want a deformed grandchild. I don't know when the deformity's going to stop. I'm going to send him back to you on a train. We'll tie him to the chair. He'll piss and shit in his diapers, but you pick him up at Union Station."

nobody's here

nobody's here
in a crooked room
there's no moon
just the bitter tears
of the disappeared
nobody's here

silence screams in silence
my mind is gone
there's no lawn
just a void
of lonely violence
watchin' fortunes fade
in the big parade

what do other people do
who share balanced lives
happy husbands
caring wives
it's hard to live without you

who will say goodbye
when it's time to die

dinner for one
holidays in solitude
no one's there
when nobody stops to care

I rode from Oregon, alone, to Los Angeles, roped into a seat, pissing and shitting the whole way. On the way to the train station, I saw a truck full of turkeys on their way to being slaughtered. It was raining, and the turkeys knew they were about to get murdered, and they were crying and whimpering in this open truck. And they all looked at me, and I looked at them, and I knew I was doomed for life. I was deformed. I was being sent back alone, a thousand miles away, alone, in the middle of a fucking war. And it was at that moment at the age of three, that I formulated the idea for a song I would one day write, a song that Jimi Hendrix recorded in 1967 called *Fluffy Turkeys*.

A thousand miles of blackouts later, the train pulls into Union Station. Mom is there, wearing Marlene Dietrich slacks, looking like some chick from the Weimar Republic.

She took me to Culver City to a foster home. Mr. and Mrs. Diamond were my new parents. Bernice Diamond was the woman's name. I never got the husband's. He was just "Mr. Diamond." He used to sit in the front room and drink himself to death. And there were twenty, maybe twenty-two children there in a giant room, all on mattresses and sleeping bags. The only food we had was Cream of Wheat. If we were good kids, we had cinnamon toast. That's all we ate. Right out of a Charles Dickens book, David Copperfield style, my pickpocket pagan-type den of madness and horror, 1942 to '46.

My mother would visit, now and then. She was under contract with Warner Brothers, a starlet. She was an also an Adrian Model and a Goldwyn Girl, at various times. She would bring me to Warner Brothers as a cockblocker, so when the guys tried to pull their cocks out when she went by to get her Gasoline Ration Card or hosiery, I started screaming and yelling when I saw the tip of the penis and she'd say, *"What are you doing in front of my little boy? Give me that fucking hosiery and my goddamn card!"*

And then she'd wink at me and I'd wink back and we'd run out of there and she'd give me a hot fudge sundae. "Well, you blocked him! Thank you."

I'd say, "You're welcome."

So imagine a crippled child, cockblocking for a Dorothy Lamour/Natalie Wood type with no talent for acting. That's how I learned how hard it was to be a woman in Hollywood and Show Business. A lot of people would accuse me later on for being a womanizer, but I sympathize with women who are pieces of meat for men in business.

My mother was an usherette at the Fox Wilshire Theatre on Beverly Drive and Wilshire, plus she was building airplanes. She couldn't provide a place for me to live. That's why I was in this foster home type of setup.

Sometime, I was between four and a half and five and a half – polio! I was in kindergarten, nursery school, when it happened—permanent paralysis. I was moved from the foster home to the hospital to the foster home. I was traumatized like rape victims and car wreck victims are traumatized. I have no memory of the rehabilitation, the treatment, the pain, the screaming, the madness, because somebody, maybe me, directed me psychologically to focus on what was going on outside of this experience. I know I came and went from the hospital. I remember the braces on my legs. We had to fight for the bathroom at the foster home. We didn't take showers because little kids didn't take showers. So I got to lie in the bathtub with the radio on, and Gabriel Heatter, who was like Walter Winchell, would talk about how the Nazis had invented this machine that was going to set fire to the oceans of the world. It was some kind of kerosene bomb or something, and I was so young that I thought that maybe the Nazis had already done it and the fire would come up through the drain and I'd be burned alive in the bathtub. I screamed and yelled and got hit in the face.

My problem was a little bit of polio. And a little bit of cockblocking.

> the lord of garbage
> has two failed actors
> as a breeding team
> these couriers disappeared
> before my very eyes
> dreams die

The only parenting I got was from the older kids. Ten, eleven, and twelve-year-olds acted as surrogate parents to us little kids. We were between one-and-a-half up to six years old.

To distract me from being a kindergarten cripple, I got to focus on newspaper drives. All the kids' neighbors would put wire around newspapers and stack them neatly on the sidewalk. Instead of the garbage man picking them up, somebody else would. They said it was for the war effort. Then there were victory gardens where vegetables were grown in the foster home garden to supplement the bad diets because of the food shortage. Then the Air Raid wardens would come and say, "Turn off your light. Japanese planes will see you reading in your living room and kill us. You can't light cigarette lighters or matches until you're adults." We were always in darkness late at night, seven o'clock on. Did a Japanese plane ever reach mainland America? They say in Oregon one crashed, but that was boogey man type gossip to keep young kids from reaching out. What a horrible time to be alive. They should make a movie of it. I hope they hire me to do the soundtrack.

I didn't see my mother again for a while. The, one day she came by in a new car, a Lincoln Continental Convertible with Suicide Doors and a big tire in the back. She was in a purple jumpsuit, calfskin. I knew something was up. Where did this money come from? I felt doomed. I felt darkness. She took me to the beach. She had rehearsed her speech.

She said, "Listen, I found Mr. Right. I found husband number two. I dumped your dad. I filed against him. I don't know where he is. He's in the Navy somewhere, but this guy is going to marry me and give me children."

"What about me?" I asked.

"You're not invited along. He doesn't want a child by a B-movie actor. He's going to give me better versions of you, because your dad is a piece of shit, and he's a better man than your dad. Nothing personal."

"What happens to me?"

"Well, if your dad comes back from the war, he'll still be your dad. Whether he comes back alive or doesn't come back at all. You know how to act in adult situations. You've been trained at Warner Brothers, cockblocking. That's good. You can fight men. You can battle people. You know how to be unloved and how to be alone. I didn't deal with you as a child. I dealt with you as an *accident*. And look, you're okay. You look fine until people see your teeth. I've dressed you up, I've taken you around and you've pulled it off. You'll be a clever man in the future. I won't see you again, because I'm not interested in seeing you. I'm gonna give this guy some kids."

I said, "Who is he?"

"He's William Friml. His father is Rudolph Friml, who wrote *Indian Love Call* and *Rose Marie* for Jeanette MacDonald and Nelson Eddy. He was the Founder of ASCAP, along with George Gershwin, Victor Herbert, Sigmund Romberg, Irving Berlin and a bunch of other guys. This is Show Business royalty. He's Jewish. I'm marrying a Jewish millionaire's son who's an Army Judo instructor. The war is over. I'm going back to live in Beverly Hills."

"Anything else?"

"Nothing personal."

"Okay. Will you drive me back at least? I don't think I can walk back to Culver City from the beach."

"Sure, I'll drop you off. Don't cry."

I said, "I never cry."

She said, "Yeah, I know."

stranded in the dark:

last message to the mother of frankenstein

bright red lipstick
burning flowers
 locked up in a mad house mortuary
 for two thousand hours

far from the desert
 far from the sea
 far from the silver screen
 far from the gold dust memories

 naked in the night
 stranded in the dark
 old lady is stone cold crazy
 out in the trailer park

under her neon moon
stranded in the dark
she's on a hospital honeymoon
out in the trailer park

three hots and a cot
said the nurse's asphalt voice
on the nut house telephone
got an ex-lumberjack daughter
got an ex-model in here
woke-up all alone
crazy momma
came on the phone
crooned to her black sheep unwanted son:
I want to go home
to be nobody
being real crazy
isn't really fun

no one spots the diva
behind the broken teeth
beneath bandages
time is the silent thief
can't anybody understand?
there's a princess of the past
locked up in timberland

suicide man
lost his piano tan
beneath the neon desert moon
post-war purple jump suit
can't spring her
from that rubber world

bad actors
black and white world
turned her to a
weak man's little girl
Joan Crawford
Frances Farmer

she waits for the final bell
all the men
that she turned down
are waiting down in hell

almost a startlet
never a star
convertibles of yesterday
headin' for the fade-a-way
atomic blonde
goin' to
the great
beyond

And then I sat there thinking, I hope my dad isn't dead. If he's alive, I'll try to work it out with him. But if he's dead, I'm going to have to learn how to be a more interesting child so I can get adopted, because that's what I hear happens. If your parents are gone, then you have to hope that someone will want you and get out of this twenty people living in one room with one bathroom deal. This is really *fucked*. This must be real life.

In 1946, my wonderful B-movie dad showed up to rescue me. I was six-and-a-half. It's an Armed Forces Sunday. Military family members are departing and arriving, and here comes Douglas Fowley with his new nineteen year old wife and a chauffeur and a body guard. My dad is a B-movie Errol Flynn. The nineteen year old is an Ingrid Bergman version of Ava Gardner.

They see me in a crowd.

"Which one of you is Kim?"

I said, "Me."

"No," he said, "which one of you is my son?"

I said, "It might be me."

"Are you Kim?"

"Yes."

"I'm your father."

I said, "Why did you take so long?"

"There was a war on."

"Okay. What are we gonna do now?"

He said, "We're gonna move to Malibu. You're going to have your own room."

I cried with joy. *Finally*, I'd have my first fucking room since my grandmother's joint.

We pull up in Malibu and there's Brian Donlevy—the actor with the moustache—

screaming at the top of his lungs. All the actors in those days had dark hair and moustaches. Well, Donlevy had a moustache. Doug Fowley had a moustache, too. Two Chorus Girls had stolen Brian's dentures.

We walk into this Malibu colony house, and my dad said, "Your room is upstairs, go upstairs." My stepmother said, "Go ahead, go up there." And I go up there, and open the door, and there's John Garfield with a Hard On, sitting on a chair, and a chick is putting Cocaine on the tip of his cock.

I said, "What are you doing in my room?"

He said, "I'm living up to my image."

"Do it somewhere else."

"Why?"

"It's my room. I have power. Go on, go, go, go…"

He says, "Okay, okay."

He hangs up his boxers, the girl turns red, takes the cocaine, walks out.

"I need some peace and quiet."

My stepmother re-enters the room and she's holding a baby. She says, "This is your half-sister, Gretchen."

"Oh yeah? You had time to have a baby? You mean that this is 1946 and this guy has been out of the war a few months ago? You had time to get pregnant and have a baby? Why didn't you come get me? I could've been the only baby. Why am I not the only child?"

"Because we're a family."

"No, we're not. I've never been in one. The only family I know is the other kids back there in the home, the twenty-two morons I had to battle every day for food, for pissing and shitting privileges. The older girls and boys kind of showed me how to tie my shoes and do the buttons and how to use the toilet. That's the closest thing I know to a family."

Well, at any rate, the nineteen-year-old left me with her tiny baby girl and my first instinct was to kill her—the baby, I mean. But then I realized I might be yelled at if I did that, so why don't I send a message to my dad and my stepmother instead? So I put her in the firewood. I had noticed the kindling when we went in there, that they had a fireplace and a cute little Hansel and Gretel bench that opened up, full of firewood. So I put the baby inside the bench, on top of the wood, and the nineteen-year-old – Mrs. Mary Fowley—says, "Where is my daughter?"

"She walked out the door," I replied.

"But she doesn't walk yet."

"Well she crawled, then. Don't bother me with details."

"What did you do?"

"You're an adult. Figure it out."

She goes and hears the crying baby, she's covered in splinters from the firewood, and she starts crying and runs down the stairs with the splintered baby, and Doug Fowley has to start acting like a dad.

So he yells, "Come down here, you little bastard!"

I went downstairs and there's Brian Donlevy and his moustache with John Garfield. They're all waiting to see how Doug Fowley is going to deal with this Homicidal Child who's been fished out of a foster home situation at the end of a war. They're smoking reefers and drinking.

Doug Fowley says, "Explain yourself."

I said, "Why?"

He said, "Why did you put the little girl in the firewood bench? Why did you yell at Garfield here about Cocaine on the tip of his fucking cock? Why are you picking on John Garfield and then trying to kill the little girl?"

"Because John Garfield should find somewhere else to live up to his fucking image. Not my room. I'm a kid. I don't understand this shit, and he can do it somewhere else, he doesn't have to do it here. And as far as the little girl's concerned, you shouldn't have waited to meet me. I'm a much more interesting child than any other child. I don't want to share any love or affection I might get from you with some stranger."

I said, "I'm gonna tell you something else."

I had figured I had to fuck with him since he was fucking with me. He wasn't talking to me privately. He was talking to me in front of his buddies. So if I didn't stand up to this guy, I would be beat. I already knew that, because I had seen movie biz males pulling their cocks out for my mom, so I realized how adult men can be to children and to women.

So I said, "Here's how it is. What have you been doing since 1941?"

"I've been in a war, and so have these guys."

"Good. I've been in a war too. I was a child left behind by a selfish bitch mother who isn't here anymore. She parked me with twenty other kids, we all ate *shit* for five fucking years. I've been in a war, you've been in a war. I'm a child in a war, you were an adult in the war. I'm still at war, you're still at war. If you fuck with me, I take a walk, and I'm a little kid, and you'll get in trouble. Don't fuck with me. Or I'll *fuck* you up. I had to battle eleven and twelve-year-olds in that fucking foster home, so I knew I needed to stand up for myself and when they turned their backs, I pushed them down stairs and I broke things in their bodies and then they wouldn't hurt me anymore."

The whole room erupted in cheers.

They said, "*Wow*, this kid's fucking *great*. Doug, this guy's a motherfucker. You gave birth to a fucking *killer*. *Yes!*"

And then my dad said, "Kim Fowley. It's time for you to go to Hollywood. Tomorrow we are going to go to Hollywood and you're going to RULE Hollywood."

Everyone cheered. I got off. I didn't get hit. I got my food. The next day, my dad took me and bought me a sailor's suit, because in those days when the parents came back from the war, the dads, if they were in the Army, they'd buy you an Army suit, or a sailor suit if he was in the Navy. So he gave me the Navy suit, got in the car, left the little baby at home—thank God— and the nineteen-year-old wife, and we rode to Hollywood.

We had two stops. First stop was Bugsy Siegel's place. They made a movie about Bugsy later. It was called *Bugsy*. But you know, there really was a real Bugsy Siegel, not a Warren Beatty version. Benjamin Siegel. He was shot dead on Linden Drive, and my dad showed me where he was shot dead and all that. Someone had shot him through the window. I said, "Why did this guy die?"

"He had no outlets for his magic," Doug replied.

That was pretty astute of Doug Fowley, because we all know Bugsy Siegel created Las Vegas and the Flamingo Hotel and was kind of a pioneer for what all that became. Culturally, he was right there, but he didn't have an outlet. He was ahead of his time. We saw where Bugsy Siegel died and then we went up to Laurel Canyon to see Bill, a photographer who was my dad's dope dealer. Bill had a studio next to a bunch of stairs that went up to the Houdini mansion.

That's where Jim Morrison—years later—wrote *People Are Strange*, looking at all the freaks going into the Laurel Canyon Market. But that hadn't happened yet. There was no Jim Morrison standing around, or Elvis or anybody else of note. It was just me, and these fucking actors.

When we got to Bill's place, he took a picture taken of me in my Sailor Suit, and then off we went to Schwab's drugstore, on the corner of Sunset and Crescent Heights. Next to Schwab's— ten years or so later—came Googie's Coffee Shop. Googie's is where James Dean used to eat with Vampira, but there was no James Dean or Vampira that day. Instead, there was Schwab's Drugstore and what they call a fountain, which is a drugstore counter where they served ice cream and cheeseburgers and whatnot.

My dad walked in and said, "Gather around everybody. I'm back from the fucking war and this is my son KIM FOWLEY."

They put me up on the counter in this Sailor Suit, and two Hot Bitches grabbed my six-year-old cock and balls. They were like nineteen or twenty, with tits and everything, and no underwear on.

I remember that. You could see everything. They stuck a candy cigarette in my mouth, because in those days, your parents were smokers, so they had Candy Cigarettes. Lucky Strike candy cigarettes had chocolate in the middle to look like tobacco.

So one is rubbing my six-year-old balls and cock and the other one is sticking a chocolate cigarette in my mouth, and my dad says, "Welcome to Hollywood, son. This is a Fag, this is a Jew, this is a Nigger, this is a Wop, this is a Bitch, this is a Hustler, this is an out of work actor—" people are roaring—"This is an agent, he's like a Fucking Pimp, this is a Publicist."

He said, "This Is Your World."

That was my first day in Hollywood.

radio wonderful and the gods
of the silver screen

all of God's children
got scared dreams
       of radio wonderful and the gods
       of the silver screen

but they got
       cool damage
       school damage
       sweet damage
       street damage

day damage
gay damage
straight damage
late damage
junk damage
drunk damage
sex damage
next damage
pretty damage
city damage
crook damage
book damage
cold damage
old damage
shock damage
rock damage

is there a rainbow at the end of the tunnel
are your troubles all rehearsed
when the lights go down on the merry-go-round
do you hear the ancient motors
or does silence make it worse?

My dad would go looking for work, and the actors used to go and stand out in front of their Agent's Offices or Casting Offices—up and down Sunset Boulevard where later, the rock and roll places would be. They would put their feet on the fenders of the car and have their shirts off, wearing a bunch of dog tags, which is to say, "I'm a veteran. I deserve a role in a fucking movie.

Look at me. I have a tan. I could kick your ass."

Eddie Hall was the best at that. He never made it. He was a version of Tom Neal. He was one of the guys out on Sunset Boulevard. He was a good guy, and my dad would ask, "What's going on, Eddie? Anybody being hired today?"

These are all guys back from WWII. All bitter that all these gay guys and family guys didn't go in The Service and they were in The Service and now they're trying to get their careers back. Turns out that dad's alleged bodyguard Nick Malnick and the chauffeur were actually sharing in the rent. Dad told them, "I'll let you guys pretend to work for me, and in reality, we're all going to Hustle Work, Pussy, Dope and everything else."

And then it came time to get high. Doug Fowley had some marijuana and he had some opium. They got some opium out of shutterbug Bill besides the grass, or maybe I'm confusing grass for opium. Maybe they were doing both, I don't know. I can't keep track of everything. I'm six-and-a-half, right? They were smoking it out of a pipe, which possibly means opium. So we walked down the street and there were some actors who had pitched in for this shit. I learned fast.

We go to Garden of Allah, which is on the other side of the traffic lights at Crescent Heights and Sunset. The Garden of Allah was started by Rudolph Valentino's wife, who had a Russian first and last name. It was an interesting place, with a big fountain in the back. This is where F. Scott Fitzgerald had a Love Nest with Sheila Graham—nineteen-twenties décor, adobe Mediterranean

Christopher Isherwood kind of modern. It was where all the New York Actors and European Refugee Types who had hidden money from Nazi Germany were staying. Or if you were about to divorce your wife, you would go there and fuck a bitch and do drugs. It was kind of an all-purpose debauched type of place.

Robert Benchley had this big luxurious penthouse in the Garden of Allah. He was an Algonquin Round Table derivative type guy who let his joint be used by people who smoked dope. He wasn't there, and these actors had the key.

My dad said, "You know what a cop is?"

I said, "Yeah."

He said, "Well if a cop comes, start waving your toy sailboat at me. Scream loudly and we'll flush our dope down the toilet. Don't interrupt my high and have a good time."

I looked through the window and he and his dope-smoking friends were all lying down with Opium Pipes.

I sat there in my sailor uniform and thought, "The father's a jerk. The mother's a bitch. I hear that when you're eighteen you can leave home. I'm not seven yet, so I've got eleven years before I split. I'll do my fucking time, and I'll watch. I learned how to cockblock from my mom. I'll learn how to hustle from this moron, and I'll try to stay sane through all this, so that when I'm eighteen, I'll find something to do with my life to survive. I gotta be careful. This is treacherous."

The cops didn't come and they all wandered down the stairs and said, "It's time to go home."

other lords ignore me
don't they know
the right tune
to raise the dead
there in my one room cemetery
I use a marble slab as a mattress
in my death bed

———

Warner Baxter had a tennis court at his place in Malibu. He had a moustache and black hair, too. On Sundays, my dad and his buddies used to go up there and do Shakespeare, wearing old clothes and smoking dope and banging around a tennis ball. Immature teenage morons in their twenties and thirties. They were trying to be kids and they were all bitter about the war. They always talked about the *fagulas*—Italian for fags—who wouldn't fight or who had too many kids so they didn't have to go. They thought that their careers were sidelined for all those years and they had to make up for lost time. That was the mantra.

At night, he would go to Preston Sturges' place, which was called The Players. It was right in front of the Chateau Marmont. I would go up there with my dad. Now, this was after his third marriage ended. If he saw a Hot Bitch, he'd say, "Go after that one." And I'd go up to the Hot Bitch and say, "Hi! Can I talk to you?" I was seven or eight by then and they'd always say, "Oh! What a cute little boy!"

I'd go, "Do you have a little boy or a little girl of your own?"

She'd say, "Yeah, I'm married."

Then I'd pull my ear, which meant to my dad, "Don't hit on her."

If she said, "Oh no, I'm single," I'd yawn and my dad would see the signal and close in. He'd come in and say, "Is he bothering you?"

"Are you his dad? What a beautiful little boy."

Then I'd take off and he'd hustle her. He'd go into the Chateau Marmont and he'd fuck her. And I'd just sit there and do my homework while he was doing that. If she was a local, he would fuck her over where she lived. And many a time, I sat in the bathroom while my dad fucked whoever he picked up at the Sturges place.

I later saw the Preston Sturges movies. He was a witty guy and made some pretty brilliant stuff. My dad wasn't a good enough actor to be in those movies, but he was a smart enough guy; he knew that if he went to Preston Sturges' restaurant he would be able to fuck some A-list bitches—which he did. He didn't fuck Joan Caulfield, though. She didn't fall for it, so good for her for knowing better.

At any rate, the Chateau Marmont was the place where, if you scored good pussy or good dope from the Allah across the street—the Garden of Allah—or at Schwab's, and you were just over at the Players, you could go spend the evening at the Chateau Marmont, which was a love nest for Clark Gable and others. And my dad would get lucky there sometimes. I lived there later. Much later.

My dad went through a bunch of wives. The wife before Shelby was Marjorie, who married Al Wertheimer, who was in the gambling business on Sunset Boulevard in the mid 1930's. Then there was Shelby, my mom. After her, Mary. And then there was Vivian, the stewardess. Then there was Joy, the schoolteacher/principal. Then there was Maryann, who was the first plain girl he married. He had goddesses after her, but Maryann was nice. There were some after them that I didn't know. I think there was a total of eight altogether. Jean was the last wife.

Kim Fowley enjoyed ten sets of parents, fourteen grade schools, and four colleges by the time he–I—headed out for Hollywood, USA as a Full-Time Street Dog.

Depending on who my parents were married to, they sometimes they had rich lives, sometimes they were poor—the acting business goes up and down, as you might guess. When my father was making movies, we lived in Beverly Hills or Malibu, Brentwood or Westwood. When he was out of work, we lived in Granada Hills, or in San Fernando, which was a Mexican neighborhood.

But here I was in 1949, turning ten.

My dad had a secret girl who was married to a man whose daughter was in my class. Sabina Kelly's mother would tell my dad when Mr. Kelly had purchased a place that they were going to tear down with a Big Wrecking Ball so they could build the freeway in the Valley. So we would stay for a couple of weeks, squatting in these places, and they'd take The Wrecking Ball and smash it through the wall. The idea was she'd tell my dad before they came and smashed it, so we wouldn't be smashed to death by the Wrecking Ball. Then we'd move to the next house on the same street for four or five days and then the Wrecking Ball would come and we'd move on. Well, it was kind of hard to live that way. In a place with no hot water and pissing and shitting on the ground, and hoping the Wrecking Ball wouldn't come.

He'd go looking for movie work and I'd go to grade school. One day in grade school, a twelve-year-old boy was picking on the other nine and ten-year-olds. My dad came to pick me up and he saw and said, "If that kid steals your lunch money, I'll kick your head in."

So when the twelve-year-old boy came to shake me down, I picked up a rock off the ground and smashed all his teeth out. My dad said, "You're my boy. You're a man now. Let's get a steak dinner." I got a Hot Fudge Sundae out of him. I used to get rewarded by my mother and father, for behaving right, with food payoffs. Every time I make money in the Music or Movie Business, to this day, I go and treat myself to a big dinner.

Well, one day, my dad and I—it was Halloween of '49 or so—we dressed up like ghosts. Like a boy ghost and dad ghost. Some of the local Mexican kids thought there was some weird shit going on in this abandoned house. We came out dressed like ghosts, screaming at the neighborhood kids and then the police came. There was a scandal, *"Out of work actor and son live as squatters, dressed as ghosts and scaring neighborhood children …"*

Then George Murphy, who was a US Senator later, got Doug Fowley a job directed by William A. Wellman, in the movie *Battleground*. I remember George Murphy bought all of his son's cast off clothes—old t-shirts and old shoes—for me to wear. Hand me downs. That movie made Dad the Photoplay Gold Medal support actor winner that year, 1950, and he got an MGM contract. We were on our way to Beverly Hills.

We got to Beverly Hills and my dad was cast in *Singing In the Rain*. He's the worst actor in the movie, but he got in it and he plays the director. That's a legendary movie with Gene Kelly, Debbie Reynolds, Donald O'Connor and Jean Hagan. Doug Fowley *sucked* onscreen. So did my mother, Shelby. She was boring, playing the Cigarette Girl (next to Humphrey Bogart and Lauren Bacall) in the Film Noir classic *The Big Sleep*.

I'm better at show business than my mom and dad. They were flawed talents. My dad learned how to get work. My mom learned how to prick tease. My mom married money. My dad married himself.

One of my jobs from age six-and-a-half to sixteen was to cue my dad, so he could memorize his lines. He would say, "You've got to deliver your lines *like an actor* or I can't memorize mine." And every time I didn't deliver the lines *like an actor*, I got smashed in the face. So to this day, I cannot memorize lyrics, scripts, phone numbers, or peoples' names unless I read them. Just like I can't do simple stuff like tie shoelaces or open a door and lock it with a key, because there were no parents to teach me how to work it out in the foster home.

message to an incomplete liar,
the dead father

you lied
about everything
your dad
the sculptor
the biker
was really the milk man
please clarify

you lied
about being
a football player
a jockey
you tried
you denied
the bad wire job
in your soul
was a
black hole

you hit me
 in the face
from 1946 to 1956
then
I knocked you out
you
did stop
to play bad cop

you
resented me
taller than you

you
were better looking
but I was more talented

you
were a ham actor
a hack
but so am I
I admit it now

you
weren't a star
you never
opened up
to anyone but
yourself

you were an
almost

you left me for
dead

fifty-seven, fifty-eight
I was gone for good
to Hollywood
 in fifty-nine

stayed away for
thirty-five years of
silence

I became the guy
you could never be
too bad you never
took the time
to know
me

So, there I am at Beverly Hills Catholic School, going to Good Shepherd Church. Dad's in *Singing In the Rain*. Happy days didn't last long. Dad got dropped from MGM, and was out looking for work again.

I started stealing wrestling and boxing magazines. Not porno magazines. I was too young to masturbate at that point. My pug dog was my shill, as usual. I was a member of the Mike and Ben Sharpe Fan Club, and my dad and I used to watch Dangerous Danny McShain and Wild Red Berry and Baron Leone and all those guys and every kid loved wrestling. Lou Thesz was managed by Ed "Strangler" Lewis. Mike Mazursky, who later became a villain in movies, was a wrestler too, and he used to come by. Also Jim "The Black Panther" Mitchell came by our place.

I worked in a wrestling and boxing arena. That was in '53, '54. I was in seventh grade. Here's what happened. One evening, my dad and one of his wives, a woman named Joy, and I, and a baby brother, were watching the 11 o'clock news on TV with a late dinner, and we saw her brother commit suicide by riding in front of a street car which cut him in half. Joy started screaming and Dad started yelling and I kept eating and the baby gurgled, and the next day Joy's father died of a broken heart, you know, the father of this dead man. And then, Joy cried and my Dad went into a Mental Hospital because he couldn't handle it.

Baby half-brother Daniel, me and Dad's fifth wife, we go down to Pacific Beach, where we lived in a garage. Dad said, "We're a grieving family. Get a job." I thought, great, I can work nights. I became the man of the house. Everyone was dying and people were screaming. I was in Catholic seventh grade far from Beverly Hills and people I had gotten to know. We needed money. I knew my way around wrestling and boxing places as a thirteen year old and I knew the lingo. I could talk about that and about baseball trading cards, among other things. So I went down to the San Diego Arena and told them a story, and they hired me to do hot dogs and hamburgers. I couldn't sell beer but I swept up and cleaned the toilets and dodged the gay child molesters in the place. I would leave there at three in the morning, have my breakfast with the Teamsters, and then go be an Altar Boy. It was 1953. Myself, I was never molested by a priest because I was too ugly. And I wasn't molested by the guys who hung out in the bathrooms at the arena, either. Everyone in the family was grieving so I was the macaroni and cheese guy, earning fast food for a family that I wasn't really a part of.

Here's a poem for seventh grade Mary Mullen, who I had a teen-age crush on.

Dracula's child

eternal, elegant
beautiful and ruined
drop dead gorgeous
she knows what she's doin'

down in the neon graveyard
Dracula's child runs naked
in the night
Dracula's child needs nourishment
hiding from the light

immortal, intelligent
glamorous and torn
smiles like a tombstone
she never dines alone

biological father
theoretical mother
thunder, fire, iron, steel
sisters of the shadows
know how the lady feels

One day I heard about Social Services. If I went to the State of California Social Services Office, they would find my mom. I wanted my mom and the rich stepfather to bail me out of my tragedy, living in a garage in Pacific Beach. One day, they found her. The new husband William Friml was not happy when he picked me up, with the mother, Shelby, sitting in the front seat of the station wagon. Off we went to their Benedict Canyon home, where I entered the eighth grade.

Kim Fowley was the Friml stepson whether he liked it or not. Court Order. Mom never told any of her friends that she had a secret child. By then, I'm over six feet tall, an ugly, drab skeleton.

Mom was embarrassed to haul me around to introduce me. William Friml had a Music Room next to the cellar room where I slept. I used to listen through the wall to him arranging music. He was an arranger of Special Material for folks performing in Vegas. That's where I learned how to orchestrate, arrange and record people who couldn't sing or play, because he was good at it. I got a job selling newspapers in front of McDaniel's Market. Jeff Chandler, Gilbert Roland—these actors were my customers.

There were ten marriages I had to live through, so every time these people were married to somebody else, there would be new grandparents I'd have to meet. Or a new brother or sister would be born and all that, I would just go in my room and shut the door and read. I used to shoplift from bookstores, I read so much. And I had an exotic English Pug Dog when Pug Dogs were uncommon. The customers in the various bookstores I'd rob would make a big fuss over The Pug and as they were distracted, I'd lift the books and magazines and put them in my school bag. So I was reading three books a week. I was reading James T. Farrell. He'd talk about when he was in the eighth grade as a forty year old man and he would've fucked a big-titted girl on the way to her confirmation class, and I'd actually be on my way to Confirmation Class, reading about how you'd fuck a big-titted bitch. "Well it says here on page 93 to do this." Good things to know when you're in eighth grade.

Kim Fowley spent his seventh and eighth grade summers in New York, in the Bronx, visiting my father's family. I heard *Sh-Boom* there for the first time ever, a momentous occasion. I explored the culinary worlds of White Castle and Horn and Hardart, and experienced the pleasures of a stoop and stickball.

Back home in September, I edited my own underground newspaper, the *Rogue's Roost*, to compete with the rival *Sodality Saber*. I started my creative writing in those days. I was in the eighth grade.

if things were different

if things were different
I might have been a scientist
I might have been in another land
if things were different
I might have been a doctor
or a hero who had to make a stand

but no matter who I chanced to be
I'd want you there with me
if things were different
you'd still be all I'd ever see
if things were different

if things were different
I could have lived on another planet
I could have flown around on a golden rocket
if things were different
I might have been an ancient astronaut
and carried your picture inside my locket

there's no use pretending
    I am who I am
and you are who you're meant to be
    but wouldn't it be fun?
to fly by the stars beyond the sun
    and see the galaxy
    just you and me

I ended up at Emerson Junior High, where
Marilyn Monroe went—and discovered that I was
a Mathematical Genius. I had my own alphabet.
I didn't need Algebra. I came up with the same
answers but I didn't need algebra. I used my
own way of counting. So they stuck me in UCLA,
in a class for gifted students. I would go half a
day. I'd go in the morning to Emerson for Ninth
Grade and then I'd go to UCLA in the afternoon.
I learned on my first day there that Education
does not equal Employment, when a graduate
student of the Mathematics Department came
back crying and screaming, "I know most of you
guys are back from Korea on the G.I. Bill, like
me. I earned this degree and nobody will hire
me, and now I'm driving a cab."

He said, "Education Doesn't Equal Employment," and slammed the door.

I said, "Oh, shit."

One of my dad's ex-wives' sisters, one of her
multiple husbands, one of my uncles, was Ray
Kline who owned the franchise of the Purple
Onion in Hollywood. So, when I was in the Ninth,
approaching Tenth grade, yours truly became
the Food Runner for Thelonius Monk, who would
go and score ice cream sandwiches down on the

corner from the Purple Onion on Sunset, where the Pioneer Chicken is now. I was the guy who got Thelonius Monk down off the bandstand when he was headlining at the Purple Onion, and took him to the Ice Cream Sandwich Shop, then got him back to the club and onstage for his next set. My Uncle Ray didn't know that the "Ice Cream Store" was where you could buy pot. Thelonius was in there smoking dope. They called it reefer. He would go in there and get high on reefer. I didn't smoke dope, but when Thelonius Monk passes it to you, you don't bogart *that* joint. He'd have the token Ice Cream Sandwich in his hand when we went back to the club.

Let's back up a bit. I never said I was Douglas Fowley's son, or William Friml's stepson. I was my own guy. I bought my own clothes, paid my own bills. Then it was time to win a scholarship to High School. I went to Chaminade before Emerson. I got thrown out for fighting. I went to San Diego State the summer before Tenth Grade to study Creative Writing under the boy preacher of England, John Theobald, who was teaching there. By the time the eleventh grade came along, I was accepted to Chouinard Art Institute as the youngest student. My dad thought I was going to be a big PR whiz on Madison Avenue and do Art and Graphics and Advertising Campaigns. He had read *Man In the Gray Flannel Suit* by Sloan Wilson and figured out that that was going to be my calling.

Kim Fowley was a Criminal Angel in high school. I was Head Pagan. Capital H, Head. Pagan as in Pagans of West L.A. One hundred and eighty teenage boys, tenth grade to seniors in High School. Eighteen different high schools. We were the first gang that went to separate schools, as opposed to one school and one neighborhood. I used to ride around in my dad's car. I'd take the hubcaps off and I'd wear a sport coat. I'd dress up like Troy Donahue. That was 1957.

Oh yeah, I was the king of all this bullshit:

TEENAGERS WITH EGGS TO TOSS GRABBED FIRST Eight kids are arrested by the West L.A. police Friday night who were headed towards the Berkeley Hill city limits. They shut off their car lights and admitted that they planned to pelt cars with the eggs. They were released to their parents' custody, advised to return to juvenile headquarters for counseling.

We changed towns. More eggs.

TOSSERS OF EGGS THROWING AGAIN Teenagers running with eggs pelted motorists in Brentwood again yesterday, according to West Los Angeles police reports a victim, last night attacked so-and-so, 17, of Grand Hill Blvd. was hit about twice by the end.

Our great moment came when found out about a club meeting where college guys would gather to discuss our high schools and how to recruit our hot girls. Our cheerleaders would all go to college frat parties and the teenage guys like us would be home alone. We had to put a stop to this. We chose the 1957 UCLA homecoming parade. They had all these frat guys that spent all year preparing their floats, where they would sit on the floats, you know, with their letterman sweaters and their football apparatus on, with our high school girls, 'cause they were scheming nineteen, twenty, twenty-one year old jocks. So we divided up a hundred and some odd Pagans, twenty guys to maybe thirty UCLA frat floats or whatever the number was, and we went and we invaded them and beat 'em all up on national TV. It got on the 6:30 news with Douglas Edwards, who was not Walter Cronkite, but he was almost as good. If you can find the Kinescope, you'll see acned rioters tripping over the floats going crazy. We had shears, and we were cutting up all their crepe paper.

RIOT INVESTIGATION ON, UNI HIGH STUDENTS TO BLAME Teenagers Riot at UCLA Homecoming. One policeman was burned by a cherry bomb in a squad car, dozens were others were bombarded with eggs, beer cans and bottles last night as some five hundred high school teenagers swarmed in the streets of Westward Village and wave of violence disrupted the UCLA Homecoming Parade.

THREE BEAT UP BOY AT BEACH A seventeen year old suffered a severe beating early Sunday, at a beach party. One of the boys picked up told West L.A. Juvenile Officers that they had first driven to a party in West L.A. only to be told that the party had been moved to the beach.

I planned it all, and before the attack my father said, "At last, you're showing some leadership abilities." And then he said, "I'll buy everyone a steak dinner if you don't get caught, and you can use the family dog it you want."

We had an attack family dog, a Belgian Shepherd named Star with a white star and a black body. A black German Shepherd is what she looked like. So with Star, the fighting dog, we headed up there and the dog barked and scared everybody and girls were screaming, "You guys are all in high school, we didn't know you were this cool! Yeah! We don't have to date these guys that are wimps!" Or whetever the word for wimps was in 1957.

NO PLACE FOR A KEG Three juveniles have been counseled and released into their parents' custody after tossing a keg into a crowd of pedestrians."

In the middle of all of this, was one of our affiliated guys, Pat Farrow, Mia Farrow's brother. He came in with a neat, fifties Ford, that he'd shot up with two hundred bullet holes, and left it abandoned right in the street.

"I won't jump on the floats, but I'll donate a bullet-riddled car," he offered.

"That would be good!" said the Pagans. He left it right in the path of the parade.

He would later die in an airplane accident, one of those Piper Club single engine planes. Great guy.

YOUTH INVADE SWANK WEST L.A. GIRLS SCHOOL Fifteen youths staged a raid at nearby school for girls last Tuesday, looting their sports equipment and smashing in a window before police arrived.

I wasn't caught. And this was before I had polio the second time. Yes, I got a steak dinner with my dad, and he said, "Those trips to the Bronx helped you." And there you go, my criminal past.

Pagans of West L.A.

in '59
we drank T-bird wine
desperate children
walkin' the line
strange boys from the white city
we wanted to dream ...
in the summer wars
we heard
the urban scream

sisters and brothers
electronic babies
an' unwed mothers
fast food merchandise
has damaged my brain

used to go cruisin'
in the atomic rain
my Buick was red

as crimson blood
I wore leather boots
in the Babylon mud

Pagans of West L.A.
rainbow warriors ready to ride
Pagans of West L.A.
stranded in time
on Saturday nite

in long hot winters
art damage made me sick
rock'n'roll heroes battin' zero
never miss a trick
pimpled killers hatin' school
after all these years
memory lanes covered
in a million dirty tears

rusty lovers an' movie kings
lost wives, lonely lives,
kids an' wedding rings
no mercy shown, no one ever cares
you lost your dreams
no nobody's there

in a life of slime
I don't get high
don't dance like a Negro
but I get by
hungry daughters

will tell you why
I've always been
a popular guy

burnin' sounds of Jerry Lee
made my army
follow me
on radio mornings
we heard the warnings
of king Chuck Berry
we gave our bodies
an' our broken souls

now I'm a night juggler
teen queen smuggler
a born liar
chasin' legs of fire
got the body language
of a nightmare dog
metropolitan double talk
lost in the fog
searchin' for hot peaches
in the Western sky
from somewhere deep in space
a magic kind of guy
goodbye, baby,
goodbye

My Pagans days were numbered. I had kicked polio in 1946. By the time 1957 rolled around, there were three species of the virus. And they told me, "Oh, you have it again."

I said, "I thought I was immune."

"No!"

"Oh, shit!"

"At least you didn't get the Bulbar strain, the one with the Iron Lung."

I had never gone to get polio shots because I thought I was immune after having it.

summertime, 1957

cast out of teenage heaven
I woke up dead
in a cold grey hospital bed
downtown L.A.
no holiday
got a freight train
burning up my brain
I can't move
body hurts
spinal cord
crushed by a thousand swords
they say I have polio
not permanent paralysis
it's here
won't disappear
no feeling
fingers
toes

neck
is a train wreck

caught the virus
from my half-brother
same dad
different mother
cement bag German nurse
wraps me in hot wool blankets
that smell like melting straw
around my stone bone body

I'm a skeleton
that glows in the dark
soon I'll be in rehab at the beach
out of reach
from my golden dreams
I'll scream
when they drop an iron horse and break my toe
I can't show fear

I'll walk again
but, I'll never be the same
the pain lingers
in feet and fingers
I'm ashamed
to be lame for life

soon I will
limp across the sand
to a long forgotten hot dog stand

to speak below the belt
to a sweaty pig, pig suntan girl
her loins
woke up dead desire
dirty fire
the rotten hunger
I thought was gone
soon I'll have her on her backyard lawn
screaming on tar under bleeding stars

I'm back
ready to attack
I'll do my hit and run
rock 'n roll crusade
riding shotgun

in the grease parade
mystery and madness
my masquerade
I deserve a solid gold Cadillac
for the dues that will be paid
I can't afford
to be afraid

tell me Lord
will you send me a baby doll
I can love
in sweaty leather
wet velvet gloves
I need touch
to be held

as I crawl alone
on this road to Hell
summertime 1957
cast out from teenage heaven
got nothing left
but the jukebox light
hope I rumble right
win every fight
on every tragic
magic night
hey rock 'n roll
bathe me in your holy light!

My father didn't want a cripple around, so Kim Fowley lived a while with a Carnation Milk heiress. Her son was in the Pagans with me. Her husband Alan Marshall had been a variation of Errol Flynn at Warner Brothers in the 1930's.

pink jaguar
red Rhonda Fleming hair

after bed pans
newly working hands
I find myself alone
still crippled
still without a home
but not for long
she suddenly appeared

pink jaguar
red Rhonda Fleming hair
she was no square
black satin underwear
we sold Indian chutney
to the new bashful brides of the west side

her son and me
we got caught selling beer and wine
the cops they promised
hard time
so we made a deal
U.S. Army or penitentiary

I said goodbye
the almost Merry Widow cried
she wasn't just my brand new mom
she and her boy
were gone for good
my final family.

I got arrested stealing wine—and selling it—
while I was living with the redhead and her son.
I was given a choice of jail time or the National
Guard. They didn't seem to care what shape I was
in. I chose the Non-Incarceration Warrior route
and headed for Fort Ord. I ended up serving in
the US Army National Guard and then the Air
Force over a three and a half year period, time in,
time out, interrupting many possibilities during
that golden period 1957-1960.

goodbye high school

no more ping pong
being young and strong
no more Pagans of West L.A.
I'm off to cold Fort Ord
to let the U.S. Army
undo the damage
of the sores
and thousand burning swords

goodbye high school
no senior prom
I'll master tear gas
I'll build a billion bombs.

———

And then began my poetry. I was out of the
Polio Hospital and fucking old women on a Lord
Byron level, with a cane. I remember going to
Venice and banging these ancient bitches. Back
then, it was Beat Poetry, Black Turtlenecks, and
Bongos. It was a whole lot of post-war angst.
Kim Fowley would go there in sports clothes and
hustle thirty-three year old woman, and people
would drink apple juice and smoke reefer and
recite long-winded poems about nothing.

I discovered the Eric "Big Daddy" Nord
experience before I was at Fort Ord. Interesting.
Nord, Ord. It wasn't a big stretch going from
Thelonius Monk, who was a Negro Smoking Pot,
to running with a bunch of Jewish Venice Pot
Smokers. Fuck that. I could deal with Eric Nord
and his friends in Venice Beach. He had been

run out of the Co-Existence Bagel Shop and had headed to Big Sur. I used to go there on furlough at Fort Ord. By then, I was eighteen and a half. So anyway, I went to the coffee house in Big Sur and there they were, the Venice guys.

"Hey, you're in the Army now!" I'd shaved all my hair. I got up there and did my Poetry Duel with whoever was around. The coffee house was run by a guy who might have been a Nazi or a war criminal, who had this hot fourteen year old girlfriend, who didn't notice me as an eighteen year old poet. Damn. But I got up there, and it was one of the Beatnik Hot Shit Gods banked against me, and he couldn't beat me, so we celebrated that night by going to Jack London's house- the famous *White Fang* author who had lived in Big Sur years before—his stone igloo hut with a dirt floor was still there and it was a place to hang out.

They said, "You've proven that you can go toe-to-toe with guys in their thirties and forties, so here, have a drink," and I fell asleep on the Copper Triangle that Jack London himself slept on. Of course, I woke up with pneumonia and found myself in the Fort Ord Hospital with Stan Bly, later to work at Challenge Records for Mel Bly, his brother, who I brought *Ski Storm* to. He and my Ski-Rock, Snow Rock records were doomed to fail, including the Rangers, the Snow Men, and the Alpines. But that was later. So, I woke up with pneumonia, and my bed at the hospital was between Stan Bly's bed, future Challenge promotion man, and the bed of one of the Lennon Sisters' brothers. There I was, stuck in Hollywood, even in Fort Ord. That was the ninth time I had pneumonia and I got it in Jack London's igloo. There's a Man Of Letters story.

So, my father took me back in, if went back to school. Soon as I got back in the house, he left the country to go film *Macumba Love*. He said, "Don't use the car. No parties. Stay in school."

One day I was heading for school and there was a girl standing there, crying. She said Buddy Holly, Ritchie Valens and the Big Bopper were dead. I heard the call. And I heeded it. February 3, 1959. That was the day I marched into Hollywood USA.

February 3, 1959

February 3, 1959
Buddy Holly
Ritchie Valens and Big Bopper died
I wasted no time to carry on
but not to take their place
stole my father's car
drove to Gold Star
parking lot
got lucky when Seals and Crofts
of the Champs
give me lunch
met Dorsey and Johnny "Big Beat" Burnett
from the Coral sea
Paul wasn't there
I didn't care

I knew I wasn't alone
'cause Buddy Bopper and Richie
were watching out for me
I felt them standing there

Danny Gould
shared the tales of Gogi Grant's sugar charts
I slept in my dad's
Studebaker Golden Hawk
far from who I used to be

is this the start
of a rock and roll broken heart
tomorrow's dreams
or nightmare screams
I will never change.

Recordsville. Kim Fowley. Rhythm and News. 1959. Kim Fowley became the Hollywood reporter for Lou Kimzey's *Dig* magazine. They had a different edition for every real city in America. The same magazine but with a newspaper insert that was local. I was supposed to find out what was big news with the teenagers so one day, I went over to Gold Star Studios and a bunch of guys were standing around outside and I said, "Hey who are you guys?"

And they said, "We're the Champs!"

And I said, "I'm going to write about you in *Dig* magazine."

That was my ticket in. That day I met Johnny and Dorsey Burnette, Gogi Grant, the fabulous

Nick Venet, and the mysterious Lou Adler. And Danny Gould, who would become an arranger and conductor at Warner Brothers.

I ended up at AIP for a while making and producing records like the Renegades *Charge/ Geronimo*. And who can forget Tony Casanova, a Ritchie Valens cousin with gold teeth, who thought the Pacific Ocean was a river? No brains, some talent. By then, of course, I was still organizing gang fights with the Pagans, but I didn't really have the time. I was busy trying to be Jewish, you know, and be in the record business. This headline is two years later after the riot, it says, *"Alert: Police Avert Planned Gang Fight…"*

It looks pretty innocent now, but at the time we thought we were being subversive.

22 cents

my second day in tinsel-town
was good
I had 22 cents
for the Hollywood Ranch Market fries
ketchup and hot water
a tomato soup surprise
two cents tax
cleaned me out
but, to my business college boy life
I was never going back

I met Nick Venet
sold his songs

made two hundred bucks
a hot piece of new hustler luck
he gave me his mom-in-law's kitchen floor
her little dog's extra sleeping bed
this Mister Zero
was starting to be a hero

safe and sound
in the little dog's bed
hey, rock 'n roll
I'm the new kid
in the land of the living dead

I got in there really fast the next morning, with only twenty-two cents. Yes, I started with twenty-two cents February 3, 1959, and by the end of 1960, we had to break into the Hollywood Argyles fan club piggy bank in order to eat Thanksgiving TV dinners for Christmas. I've lived in hundreds of dirty rooms from 1959 until now, and none of them were mansions. There have been thirty-nine American cities and twenty-two foreign countries, that I've lived in and it was always guest rooms, store rooms, the back of cars, vans, echo chambers and recording studios. Even the Communist Party Headquarters in Helsinki, Finland; where I was sleeping on plywood over hand grenades. I slept on a chihuahua's bed in 1959 at Nick Venet's place. I've lived like an animal and a dog since 1959.

From 1939 to 1959, it was foster homes. Ham actors. I mean, one dirty room blends into another one—one *Oliver Twist*, one *Down And*

Out In Paris by George Orwell, one Human Bomb Shelter situation folds into another. I mean all these things are interchangeable, institutional, awful places. I've lost more girlfriends—I mean, nobody wants to live with me. Nobody wants to hang out with me. My bands used to get nervous when they came to my living room to write songs, because I don't live like people. I live like a dog because I'm always afraid of going broke and running out of money and inconsistent incomes.

So, you live as cheap as you can. And then if you find a new guitar player, or a new movie idea, or a new singer, then you can go make the recording, or the movie, or the song, without asking somebody's permission. Because most people in America live beyond their means. They live in houses full of beautiful furniture, and curtains and all that shit. And they're slaves to their mortgage. I never was. I was the opposite.

I lived like a dog so I could dream like a wise man.

before I'm buried alive

hey, Frankie Lymon
Mellow Kings
Del-Vikings rule
this sunshine fool
Bo Diddley
Jerry Lee
your jungle jam
will set me free

will set me free
before I'm buried alive
in an outhouse toilet
on an asphalt meadow
in some far off
future Hell

I crave
to be saved
by the chimes divine
Whispering Bells
I need you now
to always
treat me well

I probably should have started singing when I was first writing for Kimzey, then I would have been Bob Dylan first, because Bob Dylan didn't have that kind of cred back when he made the pilgrimages to the hospital to see Woody Guthrie in '61. So I beat him to The Beat by four years. But I never said I was wired completely right.

And then I did meet Bob Dylan. He played guitar for me and I was quick with the lyrics and that "ehhh" voice, all of that '65 stuff. The same night he played guitar for me, he was photographed for the back of the Byrds' *Mr. Tambourine Man* album across the street.

Dig Magazine and Jan & Dean

Dig Magazine and Jan & Dean
came and went
my boring job at A.I.P.
helped me pay my rent
Marty Melcher and Doris Day
came along and saved the day
50 bucks every week
felt like a holiday

I was a flack
did A&R
signed Biz Johnston
before Rip Chords and Beach Boy lords
helped make him a star
but, Dig Magazine and Jan & Dean
didn't take me far

my growing madness
slow burning sadness
was the demon driving
me to be
a West Coast Street Dog shooting star

I realized I was too young to be a poet, but I could do the rock and roll thing. Because I was a writer, I was able to write for *Dig* magazine as the Campus Reporter. Fifty-five dollars a month—

they sure paid good. The editor, Lou Kimzey was gay, right? Well if he wasn't, he was sure working at it. He tried to have long fingernails, and he was kind of spotty faced. I went in there and hustled him, you know, before I went to business college. I remember he had Jerry Wilson on the cover. Jerry Wilson—Lou Kimzey thought he was going to be the next big thing. Well, you'll see me in *Dig*—Recordsville.

Steven Stills once said in front of Skip Battin and Van Dyke Parks, "Kim Fowley, you're as good a lyricist as John Lennon." And then I did an album with John Lennon. Flashing lights at outdoor festivals? I invented that. The first time it was ever done was at Live Peace Toronto, 1969.

I'm probably more talented than the people I produced. But they could sing, or they were girls. Or they had black curly hair. Whatever it took.

> *the lord of garbage*
> *suffers alone*
> *when the phone rings*
> *he hears*
> *the angels sing*
> *to a demon*
> *down in the darkness*
> *looking for a ride*
>   *to ride*

The making of Jan and Dean is a long, exhausting story and I believe there is another telling of how they began, a version that Lou

Adler—their manager—tells. It's fairly accurate, except Nick Venet took me over there and said, "You should hire this guy, Lou, he's a great Talent Scout and he's gonna make it in the business someday."

I met up with Adler on the way to Fort Ord, dragging a duffle bag. I told him about Jan and Dean. I told him they were gonna be the California version of the Everly Brothers. They had been Jan and Arnie, had evolved into Jan and Dean, because Arnie didn't want to continue. He went into the Navy full-time, and ended up working for Gas Money.

"If anything comes of this," said Adler, "you'll get a job here working for us." Then of course, something happened—Adler signed them. I furnished the phone number of Jan Berry, and the psychological way of approaching his dad, William Berry, who didn't like his son being a Rock And Roll Dreamer. He wanted him to be a doctor. So Lou had to work around the dad. But I gave them the heads up on it so that Lou and his production partner, Herb Alpert, would know how to deal with it.

And I told Lou, "These guys are the Everly Brothers. Tab Hunter lookalikes who make doo-wop records."

One time, Jan and Dean wanted to beat up Roger Williams, the guy who did the *Born Free* soundtrack, because they thought he was gay. They thought they could pick on him on a gay harassment level at some big rock show, and he turned to them and said, "Excuse me, but I'm a decorated veteran," I'm paraphrasing here, "I'm a Black Belt in karate. I'm a veteran of the Korean

War. I can use this on both of you and hurt you severely. Leave me alone, please."

They backed off. But they thought he was gay. I don't know if he is or was, but you know that kind of redneck, frat house, gay-hating kind of shit—that's what Jan and Dean were like.

I was amused, but I thought, "good for him."

This guy was serious. "Oh, you want to fight? I'll kill you. You didn't kill anybody in Korea, *I* did." He didn't say that but that's what he meant. And these two guys stopped giggling and laughing. It was a serious moment. Then of course Lou Adler walked in at the tail end of it, and didn't quite know what was going on.

And then they saw me. "Hey, let's pick on Kim Fowley. He's a jerk."

This was at the Earl Carroll Theatre, which was called something else back then, and was across the street from the American Recording Studio where I had the Hollywood Argyles and their road crew staying. Tough guys. You know, the Hollywood Argyles carried shotguns, knives, revolvers and everything.

So I yelled, "Hey Rube!" which means you're in trouble at the carnival, and they came over to back me up against Jan and Dean. Suddenly about eight to ten guys come over there, saying, "Hey, what's happening?"

"These guys feel like fighting," I said.

"Oh yeah? Oh, look who it is, Jan and fucking Dean. Yeah, oh boy. You guys are tough."

Some of those Hollywood Argyle people—the road guys—were rednecks, gun-toters. Ready to fight. Mexicans and hillbillies. There was one guy named Kareem Singh who really liked me and Gary Paxton. He was a Hindu rockabilly guy. He was ready to get brownie points for beating them up himself. He led the charge right across the street. We were outside by then. The theatre had a kind of like canopy over the red carpet. The whole Roger Williams harassment happened there. Jan and Dean backed down because they didn't want to fight these guys.

Jan Berry was a vicious, mean guy. Dean Torrence was a pleasant guy who went along with it. Jan was a musical genius in a doo-wop, rock and roll way. He pioneered lots of stuff. We all know about that, but he had a mean side and he was vicious. Because he was a Rock Star and had a high I.Q. and was talented, he thought that was his excuse to be a pig.

And every now and then, people didn't want to deal with that.

So Lou Adler had kinda kept his word. I learned the record business, all right. I learned how to be disappointed and how not get the promised rewards, and how to learn from all the mistakes, i.e. get it in writing, whenever possible.

Alan Freed

Arwin Records
won't let me be
a V.P.
at 19 and a half years of age
so, I said goodbye
much too dumb to care

but, much too numb to cry
so I woke up
in a Gas Station
next to a studio
ready to go
to find my spot
in the sport of rock 'n roll

a brown T-bird
rolled in one day
it was Inga and Alan Freed
I welcomed them to Hollywood
asked if they wanted information
was there a
need to hire
a jerk like me

he said, "yes"
I passed his test
I was street
quick on my feet
I worked every day
at KDAY
ran for food
filed records
kept my mouth shut
I played along
I met Paul Gayten
Leonard Chess
dated Jo Ann Castle
helped Inga Freed

buy a sundress
Alan taught me this:
"if it's not a hassle
it's not a hit"
Alan Freed invented the words:
"rock 'n roll."
he taught me to use only three sets of hands
if I needed to save an ivory track
with hot sauce
and, in the pocket, soul

Back then, of course, Alan Freed arrives, and his Thing was Records. Alan used to say, "Can't hide a miss, can't hide a hit."

Kip Tyler and the Flips happened in '59. Kip was from back East someplace. He wore leather. He was a rockabilly, but it was acquired rockabilly. Not Southern rockabilly.

I believe he was on Decca first and then showed up on Ebb later. Somewhere in between Decca and Ebb, he became the singer of the Sleepwalkers and called himself and the Sleepwalkers, "Kip Tyler and the Flips." Sandy Nelson drumming, Dave Shostal played sax, Bruce Johnson on piano, and Mike Deasey on guitar—who later went and played on Duane Eddy's records and gigs, and occasionally, Phil Spector.

Kip Tyler didn't like me. He thought I was a nuisance because I was the supposed pimp/manager of the Sleepwalkers. I got them all their gigs—Catholic school dances in Brentwood, across the street from a Jewish synagogue and we'd play shows for them, and girls school parties—all of that. And then he came along and started fronting as a lead singer, and he got the gigs.

By then I was nineteen, and was on my way to the Army, which was when the non-fabulous former Coral recording artist Jim "Kip" Tyler grabbed the Sleepwalkers and cut She's My Witch on Ebb. And then they had a falling out—Kip and the band—and in '59 I took what the band (minus Kip Tyler) had recorded to Doris Day and Marty Melcher's Arwin Records. It got released as Bruce and Terry. I also delivered Bruce Johnston to Arwin as a writer and he signed with their publishing company, Artists Music, later run by Terry Melcher. Terry was later the Rip Chords producer and sang as Terry Day. Bruce stayed with Arwin during his entire writing career. So many hits —*I Write The Songs*. Massive. He wrote *Disney Girls* for the Beach Boys—he's still in the Beach Boys! Thank you, Kim Fowley.

Between stints at the military bases. I started hustling in the record company world. Kip Tyler couldn't bark at me anymore, because in the Army I learned how to beat the shit out of people like that guy. I mean, get in my face, I'll use Army judo on you or an M1 rifle butt or something.

The last thing I heard Kip did was produce Sandy Nelson's follow up of *Teen Beat*. He didn't go back to Art Laboe and Original Sound where he recorded. He went over to Imperial. Kip Tyler did the hustling. Kip Tyler brought Sandy Nelson to Lew Chudd, *Big Noise From Winnetka*.

Kip Tyler got paid off with a token single on Imperial, *Rocket Round The Universe/The Goblin Trot*—if I remember right—which didn't do any business. Then Sandy didn't do another hit there, but he stayed on the label because they started doing albums for Imperial of instrumental versions of the current hits, which didn't have albums in those days. I did the research. That was one of my gigs over there. I was a Producer, Talent Scout and Tune Researcher at Liberty, Imperial, and World Pacific. All owned at the time by Al Bennett, before he sold two of the companies to United Artists. And United Artists was acquired by Capitol. My research showed that Cliff Nobles doing *The Horse* was gonna be a hit, but they wouldn't get their album out in time, so we had the Ventures cover it. And then they had it on one of their albums and when people wanted to buy *The Horse* on an album, it was on the Ventures version they were buying.

All the one-hit wonder instrumentals got covered by Sandy Nelson and the Ventures. I even did it myself on the *Born to Be Wild* album. People like *Born to Be Wild*, but they didn't want to hear the singer—so I did my version. *Born To Be Wild - The Exciting Organ of Kim Fowley* with three girls on the cover and me, in leather. But that was in '68, so we've now arrived in '68, we've jumped from '59 to '68 and we show that Kip Tyler made a journey, and then he was never heard of again. Maybe he's at a gas station somewhere in Wyoming and they have him doing windshields now. If you need an oil change…

> *to all this splatter*
> *there is no lady garbage*
> *the lord of garbage*
> *will have no children*
> *my children will*
> *become my songs*

Paula and Paul had a big duet, *Hey Paul, Hey Paula*. Ronnie Dawson played the drums on that. It's one of those records you wish you made because it only cost a hundred dollars or less to make, and you say, "Damn, where do you find these people? I wanna have them."

Again, I was in a hotel. Some musician was staying at a hotel across from Mae West's house, a sleazeball joint by a golf course on Rossmore Avenue. I went in there—somebody was driving 'cause I never had a ride. We dropped off the musician there and in the hall, in the lobby, was a guy and a girl, one as tall as Paul and one as short as Paula. They were real geeked-out in raincoats and polyester clothes, like janitors would wear, and I said, "You look like I imagined Paul and Paula to be. By any chance do you sing?"

"Yes! We've come down here to be discovered."

I said, "Sing! Right now."

They sang the Paul and Paula song. They were a Paul and Paula copy-duet-karaoke duo from Oregon. I said, "I will take you to the studio now and record you."

I put the musicians back in the van, called up the studio, where I did *To Die Alone* in, which was owned by a husband and wife team, another duet, Evangelical type persons. We did *No More* by the Uptones there, and Mo and Jo's record *The Yo Yo Song*. It was piano, bass and drums. Or maybe just guitar and drums, but it was something pretty minimal. Whatever it was, it was a handful of musicians and these two morons. I believe I wrote the song on the spot, and I think I hummed it to them and they sang it.

The bass line was done in a primitive way and it took about three hours.

Arwin Records paid us two hundred fifty bucks for it and buy-out points. They got the publishing and it came out and failed, of course. But the fact that they were trying to imitate something ridiculous, and that they themselves were ridiculous, and that we all thought we were repeating history because of what they looked alike and their size, it was all based on tiny and giant, but it didn't happen twice. It came out as Ronnie and Bonnie *Love Letters Never Sent*. That record just sank without a stone. It was sandwiched between Rituals records on Arwin – the other Rituals and my *Surfers Rule* Rituals. In those days you would make a record for that reason—the ridiculous factor—and someone would buy it for that reason and put it out and actually try to promote it.

Doris Day fits into Kim Fowley's life in the following ways. She was married to Marty Melcher and he had Arwin Records. The general manager was Al Kavelin, during the Jan and Arnie era and the *Chi Hua Hua* by the Pets days. Kavelin was gone by the time I showed up to work there in '59. He had left to form Lute in 1958.

Doris Day used to come to the office and I wasn't allowed to talk to her. Nobody was. We said, "Hello, Mrs. Melcher," and that's all. She was Marty's wife and Terry's mom. Marty was his stepfather. Terry went on to sing with Bruce Johnson and the Rip Chords.

I brought Bruce Johnston to Arwin. I brought other people to Arwin, who they then churned out. I brought in Ned Miller, who had *From a Jack to a King*, and they turned it down. I brought Sandy Nelson in. I brought in Johnny "Guitar" Watson—sort of brought him in—but he said, "Nah, I'd go there, but I just did a deal with King Records." So he didn't come.

And I had the Jaguars over there at Arwin, who were doo-wop gods. They were white, black, and brown and that was too much for Arwin to handle. I had Grady Chapman, Milt Grayson kinda people showing up and, you know, I was a nineteen and a half year old guy trying to bring all of unsigned California into the office. I tried to bring in *How Will It End* by Barry Darvell but they didn't go for it. And it was a minor hit—Number 101 in *Cashbox*.

Kim Fowley is lost between being an artist and a businessman. I'm neither one. I'm kind of in that grey area. So part of me is really astute, the other part of me is a moron, and the other part is a madman. When I have clarity, I can find rock and roll money anywhere. But Arwin was a place where I learned to be Jewish. I learned how to do business. I learned the difference between wholesale and retail.

I learned my dietary laws, too, so when Leonard Chess invited me to eat, at the urge of Alan Freed in '59, a year later, I knew better than to put a chocolate milkshake next to a cheeseburger with my grimy hands.

Alan Freed was a substitute father for me. He made it possible for me to eat twice a day. I got two meals a day from him—and the use of his T-Bird. He was so cool. He made records. He was a record producer and arranger and he knew his way around a recording studio. Alan didn't have credit as a record producer on some of those vinyl final records, but he knew his way around a studio.

I learned a lot from him because I could fight, though I had had polio. I had done my Army stuff, and later Air Force and National Guard and Hand-to-Hand Combat. And even as a guy who was frail, I knew all the pressure points and I could tear people apart any time I needed to.

When Alan did Record Hops, I would show up, and if people got in his way, they got hurt. That was one of my jobs. To make sure that Alan escaped intact, in case there was a hostile bunch. Sometimes people didn't know why a guy in his forties was showing up at the record hops—and they'd try to fuck with him. At the time there weren't very many hops like Freed's, but a couple of times there were black people and brown people—then here was this white guy and his goddess wife, Inga, who was a fabulous Swedish-American woman he married. She looked a lot like Elke Summer, only more voluptuous. At any rate, I made sure that they didn't get hurt. And I was there when some rednecks from the block weren't sure why a white guy would be hanging around black and brown people.

hot rod memories of the drag race derby and the Dairy Queen

back in the days of Elvis drive-ins an' the jelly rolls

jukebox queens an' pony tails
set fires in our souls

draggin' the line in our leather jackets
playin' it real cool
burnin' up like a torch inside
tryin' not the play the fool

those were the days
when we were cool an' clean
long before our wives an' kids
an' everything they mean
we're The Hot Rod Memories
  of the Drag Race Derby
and The Dairy Queen

back in the nights of Jerry Lee
T-Bird wine took you to a far-off place
every kitten checked her cat
for the sign of a lipstick trace

goin' through the motions in blackboard jungle
roarin' through the night
Ssearchin' through the shadows
tryin' to find the light

through the windows of our past tomorrows
we had a vision from the past
we had to last an' if moved too fast
we'd ever get to where we were meant to be

I was a food-runner at the Watkins Hotel before I went to AIP. Dee Clark used to like Jewish food, and I'd have to go in my dad's stolen Studebaker, and get the right Kosher food for him and his friends at the Watkins Hotel. I didn't mind Jewish food, but to those guys from the ghetto in Chicago, to them it was to them amazingly exotic.

Another person who fed me in those days was BB King. He and his wife cooked dinner for me one Sunday because there I was, in a suit and tie, hustling at the Watkins Hotel. They thought that I was interesting, and I told them that I wanted to be in the Music Business and they let me eat and talk about it. BB King can cook—really tasty food!

> *this lord of garbage*
> *eats with his dishpan hands*
> *greasy fingers rip apart*
> *the chicken's heart*
> *letting the grease roll down my chin*
> *I keep it all within*

I met Arch Hall Jr. in '59 over at Arwin. Arch Hall had a suntan and good hair and he used to go fishing with a bow and arrow and catch fish without a fishing line. He's a guy whose dad was quite the promoter. Pleasant guy. He was from Palm Springs. Norman Ratner brought him in to Arwin. Norman later produced *Hey Joe* by the Leaves. His father owned a rug company and was on TV a lot. I think Norman wrote the jingle for it in school. Performed it, maybe. Anyway, I remember Arch Hall Jr. as a Jan and Dean version of Fabian on a redneck level with some B-movie drive-in creepy crawly overtones.

I was stationed in Idaho in the summer of 1959 and got a job as a disc jockey, playing records every night as "The Voice Of The Treasure Valley" on 1140 AM KGEM—10,000 watts out of Boise. We broadcast five nights a week out of the Howdy Partner Drive-In, which was right next to the Miramar Dance Hall where Paul Revere and the Raiders got their start.

When I got out of the first long Army stint, I got a gig at Arwin, and Bruce Johnston got a lifetime agreement there and he wrote *I Write The Songs*, later to be covered by Barry Manilow, but between that day and the day that I sold Bruce Johnston to Arwin in 1959, he was a Rip Chord and a Beach Boy.

And after a year of bleeding in the streets of Hollywood, which is depicted in my poetry, I got a Number One record, at age twenty and a half, with *Alley Oop*. It came and went really quick.

Sandy Nelson lost his leg after his great success with hit singles *Teen Beat* and *Let There Be Drums*. Those were his two hits and he had a pile of hit albums and he was a session musician on Phil Spector records, and he sang on *Alley Oop* and did percussion, and there's some other stuff I'm not familiar with. Tremendous drummer, really great guy, and then one day he had an accident and he lost his leg. He carried on, but I don't know what's happened to him.

from the ice cream scoop to: Alley Oop

in the Pacific Palisades
there was a girl magnet store
called the Ice Cream Scoop
across the street from The Hot Dog Show
I used to cruise for surf beasts there
in my madness glow

Mary Hughes
of the beach party movies
was the neighborhood surf beast star
this is what I was doing
cruising in nameless rusty cars
I still hung at state beach
with guys from West L.A.
but, I was a Hollywood cat
still joined at the hip to the world of sun
it was time
to start my climb
to the top of the pile
time for Kim
to be number one

a year after I arrived
I collided with good luck in overdrive
I was asleep in my Gas Station cot

when I heard Dallas Frazier loudly knock
on the door to use the John
then I heard his song
from the great beyond

Alley Oop went to number one
out sold Elvis in 1960
I looked like I had won
but, Gary and the Argyles joined me
in spending every lucky cent
went back to being broke
hardly enough to pay our rent

so went back to the Ice Cream Scoop
a has been at barely 21
it was easy come, easy go
so, I gobbled down
ketchup and relish at
the Hot Dog Show.

———

Kind of anticlimactic, wasn't it? *Alley Oop* was a single, you know, and they gave us twenty-seven thousand dollars in royalties, and the follow-up stiffed. We had to buy a station wagon to haul the fucking band around when they did one-nighters, and one day the money was over. That's what we got, that was it, we broke down. We broke into the fan club piggy bank to have cheap Christmas TV dinners in December of 1960. And then we sold the publishing to Bobby

Darin's T.M. Music. That was it.

Bob Keane was another ex-bandleader who had a great line, "Hey! I think you're a talented kid. Come into my office and tell me what your dreams are in rock and roll. Listen, I'll put your record out, just sign here. Gee, we're gonna have a great success!"

Kid says, "Wow, what a great guy."

Nice as can be, brilliant, talented, clever. No money, honey. Ever. And he put out wonderful records. Look at that stuff, tremendous. I was the Art Director for Del-Fi for a month before *Ally Oop* broke. I designed album covers. I went to art school, too, Chouinard Art Institute, now CalArts. I went in there at Del-Fi and said, "Put that here, put that here, use this color, use this font, okay next one." Boom, boom, boom. There was a mechanical guy doing it and I told him what to do, what colors to use and where to place all the lettering and shit.

Here's a National Guard Blues poem.

combat

none of us has ever gone to war
no cargo planes
no burning garbage
no fire in the cake
no unholy voices
baby, I've been freakin' again
I saw you on a calendar
you was wearin'

sweet mysteries of endless battles
the hangouts and hangovers
of a lavender sea
in a lone star universe
during one of them outlaw nights
where there's bonfires in the neon
after you meet me after work
with fire power
love's on my side
on the hardcore bitter edge
in man made
melody line
nobody's fighting
there's no water
no meat, eggs, fish or milk
somethin' ain't right at the beer gardens
and
I'll never meet Eastern Europe's newest
sex symbol

I was in the International Guard then. Around '61-'62, there was some shaking and rattling going on around the Berlin Wall. That's where this poem comes from. I was all excited about being in the war, and then all of the sudden I'm, "Oh, well." That was my response to combat. Dick Dale was in the Guard, too, when I was there, but I didn't know him then. I knew his father later, after my time in the National Guard, because he was around in '62 over at Rendezvous, which distributed Deltone, and they were just recording there. So I used to see the father, who was just like Colonel Parker. He was a really good manager.

Dick was a fireman in the Guard, and I was doing two things. I started doing Court Marshals as a Court Typist. Then I went into training Jet Jockeys with high blood pressure to grow up, be mature and then fly a slow airplane. I was the one in charge of grading them. I had to memorize the cockpit. So if you're ever in a 1961/62 transport plane and the pilot passes out, and I'm in the plane, I know the cockpit. I can't find my way to the post office or the supermarket, but I can land an airplane, according to the Air Force National Guard anyway.

the silver sixties

from Benedict Canyon
to the streets that moaned
even the stars that shone
had to stand alone
from the studios
to the eyes that cried
even the heavyweights
had lonely nights

from the bungalows
to the gigolos
even the boring ones
craved the frozen nose
from the limousines
to the ones who failed

even the great ones
spent time in jail

from the mansions
to the hotels
even the phonies
wore it well
from the doctors
to the dealers

———

You never know who you're going to meet when you're young and crazy. I ended up in a mansion on St. Ives Drive, living with a woman who was my dad's age—born in 1911. Every thirteen days she'd let us have a wild party. She later formed Del-Rio Records. Me, and Skip Battin from Skip and Flip (later of the Byrds) lived there. Flip was Gary Paxton. *Cherry Pie* was the last record those two made together. The three hits were *It Was I, Fancy Nancy* and *Cherry Pie*. The great lost Skip and Flip single is *Over The Mountain*. I don't know why that record never came it. It was tremendous, cut at American Recording after *Alley Oop* had taken off. They put out *Doubt,* which wasn't any good and I didn't like, and *Teenage Honeymoon*. There were more, later Skip and Flip records, but with different Flips and different Skips, all for Bob Shad's Brent label.

So, we would have wild parties every thirteen days. We had Prime Minister Nehru of India up there, rocking. And he was a friend of Richard Neutra, the famous architect who lived next door, contemporary of Frank Lloyd Wright. He was there, too. Did they smoke marijuana? I'll never tell. But everybody else did, maybe they got a Contact High.

In 1961, New Years Eve, I threw a party for Joey Dee, minus the Starliters. The Marketts were there, and Rod Lauren, who was at RCA Records, and PJ Proby, when he was Jett Powers.

Little was I to realize that in 1961, I'd only have one hit. Paul Revere and the Raiders *Like Long Hair,* which I co-produced with Gary Paxton. Mark Lindsey sang the song *Sharon* on the B-side. He didn't sing on the instrumental sides of the singles even though he was supposed to—he was asleep underneath my bed, 'cause he needed a place to sleep.

Then he drove me around in his car like a chauffeur. I always like to say that two famous chauffeurs in rock and roll were Mark Lindsey of Paul Revere and the Raiders, and the other is Danny Hutton from Three Dog Night.

After that, I was rooming with Derry Weaver, who wrote *Moon Dawg,* plus he played guitar later for the Hollywood Argyles. He was a white guy who was part of the Argyles road band. They'd been on Lute Records. The Hollywood Argyles recording group was half Black, and in those days you couldn't have a mixed group. And so you had white guys imitating black people and going on the road. By '61, nobody cared about the Hollywood Argyles. We tried to revive the Gamblers with *Teen Machine,* on my label, Last Chance Records. By that time, Mark Lindsay was the third roommate, and in order to pay our bills, we used to have girls come over to worship Azor, who was this red light bulb, and we had piano wire under the carpet connected to the light bulb. We used to tug on it making it move—*"Azor, should the girls take off their clothes, or give us money for food?"* Depending on what we felt like doing, Azor would awake and we'd get either sex or money.

Kim Fowley and Skip Battin skipped out one time and went to New York to deal with Dick Clark and the night time version of American Bandstand. We were hanging around the clubs and saw his tremendous group called Mel Smith and the Nite Riders. These guys were better tan Ike and Tina Turner who were on the same label, Sue Records, Juggy Murray's label. They were better than Bo Diddley. They had a human skull in lieu of a cowbell that was reinforced with copper. So you heard the sound of the stick whacking a human skull. We thought, man, the Hollywood Argyles have a record that's Number One, but no way could they complete with dogs like this onstage.

The Rivingtons were the Sharps. They did all the yelling in the background on Duane Eddy's hits. They had a single on Guyden called *Gigglin'*. They were a b-minus spinoff of the Jesse Belvin neighborhood era of the Coasters cum Gaynel Hodge/ Hollywood Flames. Gaynel Hodge co-wrote *Earth Angel* and played piano on *Alley Oop*. He was also a wonderful guy who was the piano player on *No More* by the Uptones. He brought me the Rivingtons. They kept changing their name. There were four guys – Al Frazier, Rocky Turner, Carl White, and John Sonny Harris. They showed up and we did *Moonlight In Vermont* and three other tracks for a Warner Brothers EP as the Crenshaws. It failed. They were the first black vocal group on Warner Brothers Records. Mickey Goldsen, Johnny Mercer's publisher, owned the *Moonlight in Vermont* copyright, and he made the deal. Then they reappeared as the 4 After 5s with a record called *Hello Schoolteacher!* By then, they had converted to Islam, the Chicago version with the bow ties and suits, not the Islam of today. They were working at the Black Muslim bakery. I acquired two Johnny Otis supervised sides for All Time Records, a subsidiary of Del-Rio Records, co-owned by KF and a female millionaire. We had a party one night, so I had them come in as the caterers, bringing in the Black Muslim bakery goods into her Beverly Hills mansion. Of course they sang and did Doo Wop and dance steps and the crowd went wild! That record failed.

I was still living in the basement of the mansion. One morning, at about 7 AM, I got a wake-up call from Al Frazier, spokesman for the band. He said, "We just wrote a Number One song!" And they sang *Papa-Oom-Mow-Mow into* my ear from a telephone booth in Griffith Park. They were hitting a pencil on the phone booth glass to show me the beat. And they said, "Produce us. You're our producer. What do you think?" I said, "I failed you as the Crenshaws producer and as the co-owner of All Time Records. Let me take you to Adam Ross and Jack Levy." Adam was a good producer and Jack worked for Beechwood Music. I called their office at 10 AM and said, "This group has a Number One novelty R&B/Doo Wop hit I want a point= 1% finder's fee. Can we come by at noon?"

don't be fooled by slogans

dad lives football, he bets on the Rams
little brother gives all night
little sister watches the married man
mom is stranded again
she doesn't have any friends in her older life
her lonely life

don't be fooled by slogans
slogans bother me
don't be hurt by propaganda
read a book
pick a flower
look into the sky
and you might see someone

you read this page
and you look out the door
and you wonder if I
know more than you do
in real life
I sit in my hotel
I wonder if I did
as well as you thought I did

I have a very strange memory. It's all visual. That's when the Rams were still an L.A. football team. Kim Fowley wrote a song called *Nut Rocker* at the end of 1961. In early '62, it was about to start climbing the charts, and I'd worn out my welcome in this big house I lived in, where the Joey Dee party happened. And so I went and moved into the Park Sunset, that's the hotel I refer to.

That's where Eddie Cochran wrote *Summertime Blues* with Jerry Capehart, who we called "Cap." He wore a yachtsman cap. He was the guy who played the drums on Eddie's records on a suitcase. The Park Sunset was next door to where GNP Crescendo would later have an office. It was a nice hotel, like staterooms in a yacht. A lot of B-movie actors lived there, like John Ashley from Hot Rod Movies, and there were a pile of AIP actors and actresses who used to, for some reason, stay there, even though they lived in other parts of Hollywood. It seemed to be the place where they could wreck hotel rooms or drink a lot of beer. It was down the street from 77 Sunset Strip, next door to the Sea Witch. I was living there. I remember the Dories came to visit.

"We're the Bel-Air Bandits on Jan and Dean records," the Dories told me. They were accompanied by Lenny Waronker, later became head of A&R at Warner Brothers. I recorded them doing *Stompin' Sh-boom*. It went to Number 18 in Hawaii, hence my time was not wasted at the Park Sunset.

I need God

you can't be
no solitary man
you need God
and sympathy

listen all my children
and faithful friends
I am so alone

———•———

Sometime late in 1962, as I headed toward 1963, I felt alone. My song *Nut Rocker* had gone to Number One in England and sixteen other countries, but it was only a Top 20 record in the States that year. The first version was by Jack B. Nimble—actually a bunch of session musicians doing *Nut Rocker*. That was the Original Version, and it was covered by B. Bumble and the Stingers later on. They were session musicians and it was on a small label called Del-Rio, which I co-owned. Then the lady who I co-owned the record label with decided that she didn't want to be in the record business anymore. On New Year's Eve, the end of New Year's day 1962, she decided to have a temper tantrum and took all the records and smashed them to bits.

She was screaming that she wanted to have the rowboat and the boat rental concession at the lake in McArthur Park. She wanted to have boats with flowers and weird colors painted on them and rent them to people who wanted to go sailing. She didn't want to be in the record business anymore. But I knew that *Nut Rocker* was good. So as she was smashing them, I rescued three copies.

I mailed one to *Billboard* and one to *Cashbox* to see if they'd give it a great review, and *Cashbox* gave it a Pick of the Week. I took the third and last copy over to Snuff Garrett at Liberty. He was a big producer there, having produced Bobby

Vee, among other people. I told him the story, that the record was supposed to be out, and that the woman had decided she didn't want to be in the record business anymore.

"Here's the *Cashbox* review," I said. "Would you please cover this?"

"No," he said, and passed it back to me.

I took the bus over to Rendezvous Records, told the story to the label owner, Rod Pierce.

He said, "I will cover this, but I'll produce it." We went and had lunch and he said, "Go for a walk. When you get back, your record will be done and you're writer and publisher."

Al Hazen, who played piano on it, he was at the lunch and said, "They're giving me twenty-five dollars for playing on this. I feel guilty taking his money because this is a horrible song. It isn't going to do anything, but apparently it got a good name, so why not?"

Al Hazen was the piano player, Jesse Sales was the drummer, and Rene Hall was the guitar player and the bass player. Rod Pierce had this magical studio in the Rendezvous office. It sounded just like the Chess Records studio, a small room with great compression qualities. I went for a walk and came back a couple hours later and there it was.

Rod Pierce said, "What do you think?"

I said, "I don't like the solo, but I like everything else."

And they put it out and it went to Number One in fifteen to twenty countries around the world. It wasn't that big a hit in America. Then the Del-Rio woman who broke all the records decided that she'd better stay in the record business, since the cover was taking off. So she ran down to Dot with the master tape. So Dot put the original Del-Rio version out, and it was the hit in Phoenix. It charted there but it didn't chart anywhere else. It bubbled under in *Cashbox*—it's a good thing I got a review copy to them back when she was smashing copies. Rod Pierce later produced Dick Dale, who liked to pretend that stuff he was doing was cut at the Rendezvous Ballroom or Harmony Park , and they might have been. But the big records, as far as I know, were done at Rendezvous Records, because Rendezvous distributed Deltone. Jim Monsour, was the genius father/manager of Dick Dale, and what a great manager he was. He and Dick owned Deltone. I'm in the Dick Dale *King of the Surf Guitar* documentary, telling some of these stories. They cut *In the Mood* with Ernie Fields in that studio. It was a magical building on Selma. Upstairs was Rene Hall's office, and Lou Rawls used to go up there to arrange his songs, and then Sam Cooke would go up there. And to the right of Rene's office was Walter Hearst's office. He was my lawyer from 1959 to 1990. He died in '90.

Pérez Prado—the famous Mambo King— would hang around the building. According to neighborhood legend, he slept in Room Seven up there and they named a publishing company after it— Room Seven Music. He slept on the floor in the forties. Another office was Aki Aleong. He had the Mighty Hannibal. That was his office at the time. Directly across from him was Fred Stryker, who was in business with Syd

Nathan from King Records and shared some co-publishing enterprises. I don't remember all of his hits, but he was in the Syd Nathan/King Records world. I met Syd Nathan around that time. What a genius he was. He had started King. I spent an afternoon with Syd, he granted me an audience.

I used to meet people like that and just listen to them talk, because you know, Syd Nathan created so much. James Brown, Hank Ballard and the Midnighters. Starday Records. I mean, whoa! And he made lesser records like *Sugaree* by Rusty York. Also the 5 Royales. Whoa! I mean, come on. When I met him, he sat there and talked. I listened. I believe he was the mentor of Seymour Stein.

I never met Morris Levy. But I met Hy Weiss and George Goldner. All of these are great record men, you know these guys, they invented lots of things. I never met Sam Phillips, but I'm in the Sun Records book. There's a Sun Records book out there and *Alley Oop* by the Hollywood Argyles is a record they listened to as a production engineering community in that studio. Apparently it made an impression and it was name dropped by some reference as a record that the Sun Records people were listening to in the context of a par of excellence. Wow, what a compliment!

> *wounded in these wars*
> *the lord of garbage*
> *swallows hard and drinks*

slowly
softly
the medicine called compromise

> *compromise*
> *is worse than the battles*
> *that have been*
>> *lost*

Sometime late in 1962 as I headed toward 1963, I felt alone. What I just remembered is that in 1962, my song *Nut Rocker* went to Number One in England and sixteen other countries. Yes, it was a Top 20 record in the USA that year. I was Number One overseas, but still being unrecognized, un-loved at home.

nightmares cold

nightmares cold
in days of gold
we're on fire
it's the grand desire

can't lose demons
we share
everywhere
in red velvet air
even in the evil ones
know someone always cares

The Red Velvet, that was a club in Hollywood. I went and slept on the floor there when Jimmie Maddin ran his Jimmie Maddin's Supper Club there. Jimmy Maddin. He produced Sky Saxon's first record. He was like Louis Prima and Sam Butera in one guy, a good-hearted guy and a good sax player. He also had a really good single on Imperial called *Tongue Tied*. Imagine if Freddie Cannon and Louis Prima and Sam Butera all were the same person.

You had to be twenty-one to get in there. In 1959, he had an unadvertised teen night, the Teenage Nightclub at Jimmie Maddin's Supper Club. I presented Eddie Cochran there the last time he sang in America before he went to England, where he co-headlined with Eugene Church. Eugene sang *Pretty Girls Everywhere*. Eddie sang *Three Steps To Heaven*. That was pretty interesting.

That location has had many different names. The last it was the Red Velvet, was sometime in the Seventies. It was one of those places where everyone wore sharkskin suits and women always had beehive hairdos. The guys all looked like Wink Martindale. I once had a poetry duel with Redd Foxx there. That guy was amazing, he could get up and go at it with anyone, you know, do a verbal duet back and forth, and he got me. I tried the duel again with Buddy Guy, when he was on tour with Junior Wells at the Golden Circle in Stockholm, Sweden in 1970. Kim Fowley got shut down again. I didn't have the pocket right.

1963 was the last year of the Surf Machine, when *Wipe Out* was the *Louie Louie* of the time and the Beatles were flexing their muscles, waiting to make that golden climb to the top of the charts and break all the hearts. There I was, next door to Capitol Records with Danny Hutton, later to be in Three Dog Night, looking into the California night while Danny was saying to Jackie DeShannon, Kim Fowley, and Jack Nitzsche.

"I predict," he said, "That you'll all be dead in certain ways, because the Beatles will take over and the theirs will be the next rock and roll days and everything up to now won't count anymore and bands will stop, and peoples' careers will grind to a halt. They'll have to throw salt over their shoulders for good luck, they'll be fucked, because Merseybeat's gonna come along and drive us all crazy in the California heat."

> *the lord of garbage*
> *thu out the universe*
> *wonder why*
> *in the middle of summer*
> *there are no*
> *shadows*
> *in the sky*

David Gates picked me up hitchhiking. He lived
on Canyon Drive, and I lived on Canyon Drive,
and he gave me a ride. I saw his instruments in
the back of his car. I said, "Are you a musician?"

He said, " Yeah."

I said, "I'm a producer"

He played me *Popsicles and Icicles*. We went
into where I was living in Nick Venet's mother-in-
law's later house from her first marriage. I don't
know if they were married legally or not but her
mother was the landlady and I rented a room. It
was the same room I lived at in '59. I went back
there in '63 and again in early '64. So anyway, he
played *Popsicles and Icicles*, guitar and voice, and
I told him, "I'll make a Number One record out
of that, I'll cover it," and he said, "Okay," and I
did. That's how I met him, hitchhiking. He was
the driver and I was the guy thumbing the ride.

Astrology by the Murmaids. Did I really have
an interest in astrology? None. It was an idea
to put *Happy Birthday* to astrology lyrics and
I thought it would sell. Well, I was wrong. The
Murmaids sang background. That's where I
discovered them.

I had *Popsicles and Icicles* done with the
Murmaids, a session I produced on June 26,
1963. It set me free, because by February 8, 1964,
I was Number One in *Record World* with it. And
then the Beatles replaced me a week later with *I
Want to Hold Your Hand*.

So, Danny Hutton was right, I finally could
understand that I had to learn again and start
again. My friends, welcome to the end of 1963,
the beginning of '64.

its 2am: it must be London

rain is falling down
like tears from the angels eyes
far from Northern skies
in these faceless crowds
my heart is beating loud

it's 2 am: it must be London
there's no cars or trains
just me and no one is here
but a million sleeping people
who all have disappeared
it's 2 am: it must be London
and the visions
and the pain
of the fortune
and the fame

its not always going to be like this
I'll win the war
I'll find the endless bliss
but for now it's just the future and
my memories that are protecting me

the moon is breaking through
the early morning dew
I've got a lot to prove
now that I made my move
all I've got to do it
believe in that is true

In 1964, I sold my half interest in Chattahoochee Records. *Icicles and Popicles*. With a suitcase full of money, I went down to Music City and bought the Beatles' Vee-Jay albums, which I like better than all the others, jumped on a plane and went to Heathrow, which is where all of the dreams grow in a London Airport Garden.

There I was, with a bulging suitcase full of Chattahoochee buy-out money and my greasy clothes and then the suitcase broke, and all my Beatles records from Vee-Jay fell on the floor. And the customs man said, "If you're going to come to England, don't bring American pressings of British hits. I thought you were coming for a holiday."

"Oh, yes sir. Just something from home to keep me company."

PJ Proby's real name was James Marcus Smith, and he showed up in Hollywood as Jett Powers (two Jetts in my life—Jett Powers and Joan Jett). He was a miniature Elvis Presley. Dottie Harmony called him "Baby Elvis." When you saw him singing on *Rocket to Stardom*, Proby looked like the actor John Derrick. He had thirty-five or forty different singing voices—he could be anything. He could be Caruso, he could be Wilson Pickett, he could be Hank Williams, he could be Elvis, he could be a Beatle, he could be anybody. He can do falsetto like Maurice Williams and the Zodiacs. This guy was possibly the best white rock and roll singer who ever lived in terms of versatility.

Going in the studio he could be any lead voice you wanted, any harmony voice you wanted and

could read off of sheet music like Sinatra could.
You didn't have to rehearse anything—here's the
song, he gets it and does it like he's been doing
it for ten years after hearing it for one minute.
Astounding. When you think of the expression
'Recording Artist,' he's the Number One
Recording Artist I've ever been in a room with, in
terms of just doing it. And onstage, he was just as
good as Jim Morrison. I never saw Elvis. This guy
was James Brown II onstage. He had the look,
the sound, the show, plus, he could write.

He wrote *Ain't Gonna Love You No More* for the
Ribbons—later covered by the Searchers. He
later wrote *Handsome Guy* about a character who
was not handsome, sung by Dick Glasser under
the pseudonym Dick Lory. It was on Liberty
Records and was Number One in Australia and
nowhere else. He was a writer at Liberty when
Randy Newman was a writer there, when Jackie
DeShannon was a writer there. They were all
down there together at a division of Liberty
called Metric Music. Tremendous!

PJ had drinking issues. He had emotional
issues. He had a high IQ—he was a great guy,
good person, too much. Too much of everything
good, he overloaded on excellence. That was his
curse, there was nothing wrong with him. And
he had John Barrymore's drinking adventures,
he was the ultimate two-fisted drinker out of any
Eugene O'Neill novel or any Irish New York play
or Detective Story. This guy was a world-class
drinker.

When the Beatles were Number One, the
Stones were Number Two, he was Number Three
in the *Melody Maker* worldwide poll. Number

Four was Herman's Hermits and Number Five was
Tom Jones, in every country in the world except
Japan, Canada and America. The only hit PJ had
here was *Nicky Hokey*—his Creedence Clearwater
approach—and he had hits everywhere else in
different styles. He's still alive as far as I know,
and every now and then I talk to him through
e-mail or on the phone. I never got to produce
him. I was his publicist and I was his master
of ceremonies on his 1962 English tours. I was
younger than he by six months. If I had been
an older guy, I could've been his manager or
producer. I possibly could've dealt with all of his
challenges, but as a guy six months younger than
him, I was his friend, but I wasn't oppressive
enough to be a producer or manager.

Jimmy Page came in one day—when Charles
Blackwell didn't show up—and we produced PJ
on something in the studio, *Alone Forgotten*. PJ
sang on the Rituals records. He sings high and
low harmony on *Surfers Rule* and on *Gone*, that's
him as the high voice. I guess I did produce PJ
Proby in the Rituals. He was as Session Singer
himself and did a lot of session work. In those
days, everybody sang on everybody else's records
and played on other peoples' records, and you
would take a vacation from your own recording
to sing on someone else's stuff just like a change
of underwear kind of deal.

I lived in the same house he did. He had his
room, I had my room, and downstairs was Nanker
Phelge, a real person—later, a pseudonym for
the Rolling Stones. But James Phelge—Jim – was
a real guy. And he would sit and chain smoke
in Proby's downstairs room, with Viv Prince,

drummer of the Pretty Things. Viv lived there on that floor. Upstairs, Bongo Wolf would sleep at the foot of Proby's bed like a faithful dog at times. And after Viv Prince left, Gary Walker showed up—of the Walker Brothers. His real name was Gary Leeds, and he took the PJ Proby formula. You know, Hollywood Failure turns into Superstar in England. Well, as far as Hollywood's concerned, he was a failure because he only charted in Australia. Proby was that mystery guy, the songwriter who would chart with *Ain't Gonna Kiss You No More* by the Ribbons, distributed by Lute, the *Alley Oop* label.

Viv Prince was a good guy. He had a good sense of humor. Imagine living in the same house with Kim Fowley, Bongo Wolf, PJ Proby and Mr. President—who was the beagle dog—and we're all buddies. You know, it was like Elvis living with the Memphis Mafia kind of a thing, great times. I was twenty-five years old by then in '64 and I was just a big idiot enjoying Beatlemania and swinging London. I should have produced PJ Proby, but there was no use because other people were. Jack Good produced him, and Charles Blackwell, and some other people. I was just having fun.

Kim Fowley doesn't always make the right business decisions. Imagine living with the Number Three artist in the world (excluding America, Japan and Canada) after having Number One records as a producer or co-producer or writer, and it never occurred to say, "Probe, why don't you and I make a number one record?"

It just never occurred to me—or him. PJ Proby did say one thing predicting my future life.

He said: "When you're an old man, the things you forgot will be the things your rivals will never even learn. And you'll never get back to Beverly Hills when you come home. It might be a block away from you, but you'll never be on the other side of the line. There's something about you that's never gonna get to back to where you started." Remember, I had parents who used to live in Beverly Hills, and he was right, I never got back. Well, I never wanted to go back, because if I wanted to be that successful, I would've had to hurt a lot of people. I was pretty brutal and abrasive as it was, and I didn't want to be worse. I'm really good onstage. I have stage presence. I could've been great, but I didn't choose to be. I didn't need that pressure of being that great live and singing. And I didn't need the pressure of being that good in show business and hurting people, because that's what you have to do if you really want to do it right. You have to break some hearts and I didn't want to do that, and I never did. But I had some of the components. Although a lot of people say I broke their heart, but that's their issue, because I never went out to deliberately hurt anybody. I only wanted to survive.

I never wanted to be a star and I succeeded. I never wanted to be rich and I succeeded. I just wanted to make a living. That's probably because I had a B-movie dad. He wasn't an A plus. He did an A plus job a few times, but not consistently. Charlie Chaplin had a father in vaudeville and he did better than his dad, and he had a mother who was a showgirl who ended up in a mental hospital and he did better than she did. I did better than my parents but I didn't do as good as I should've done. Sorry about that.

I could've done better. When I'm dead—three to five years after my death—everyone will find out how good I was, because I have a lot of things like these poems and lyrics. I have the musical equivalent of this stuff, stuff that hasn't been released or stuff that hasn't been available for release at this time, but in the future, look for it.

So, I worked for PJ Proby. I was the Court Jester, the MC, and occasional ghost producer, fellow seducer. Brian Jones, Graham Nash, Lulu all came to the house. We were all Sperm Supermen. It was swell.

Ritchie Blackmore. *Earthshaker/Satan's Holiday*. In 1964, Derek and Lawrence brought Blackmore in with a drummer and bass player. They had been playing with Joe Meek's group, the guys who backed Heinz and artists on Joe Meek's roster.

So I said, "You guys are going to be England's first surf instrumental band." We did the session at Olympic Studios with Keith Grant engineering, who had just done the Rolling Stones *Come On*. *Satan's Holiday* by the Lancasters came out on Titan in America. Cleveland had a John Zacherle kind of midnight monster movie host called Ghoulardi who played *Earthshaker* on his show a lot. We used to get these big checks from BMI for writing that thing, probably because of the Ghoulardi thing.

Joe Meek, 1964. Kim Fowley called him up because I was a fan of his records and I told him who I was and what I'd done and that I wanted to come out on a pilgrimage to his place in North London. I took a cab there and the door opened and there was Joe Meek.

Joe Meek and Elvis Presley both had translucent skin, their skin glowed. You know, Elvis Presley in person, his skin actually glowed. Like a halo or something. And Joe Meek had that same translucent, glowing white face, except unlike Elvis, his face was like a turkey. You know for Thanksgiving, you go in the market and the frost or mist on the turkey wrapper when you look through at the meat? So he had the translucent face with the mist on it, as opposed to sweat. And he had this immaculately furnished kitchen.

We went in the kitchen and he said, "I record here, near the stairs."

The same stairs where the Honeycombs would do *Have I the Right?* Wow. They hadn't done the record yet. He'd put the drums on the stairs. And then he had his budgie, which is what he called his parakeet. He said, "Well, the only problem with recording at home is if I forget to put the towel over the bird cage, my budgie will start doing parakeet songs during the recording, so I have to put the towel over the bird cage."

I got lunch out of him, and it was a turkey sandwich, which matched his turkey face. White bread. He made it himself. We sat there and ate turkey sandwiches and I told that him it was great meeting him and we both complimented each other on respective records, and off I went. He was an analytical guy. He had on a Mr. Rogers sweater with buttons on the front, and he had rock and roll cream on his hair, with a translucent turkey-in-a-supermarket mist on his face.

I don't know if Joe Meek and Phil Spector ever met. No, they both had separate-sounding records. Lee Hazlewood taught Phil Spector about sound, so that's where Phil Spector got it from, and then from various other people in New York when he went back there. There's speculation from me that possibly Burt Burns taught Phil Spector a trick or two, because he was active at the same time. Before he and Phil Spector got famous as producers, they possibly worked on similar records. Around the same time, Jerry Wexler was sponsoring both of those guys.

I wasn't exactly friends with Phil. We were acquaintances. I knew his sister Shirley was good-looking from her hanging out at Mama Yuro's spaghetti place with Phil. That's where Troy and Timi both would perform as brother and sister, although they weren't. They were just the same size, and looked alike, so they passed for siblings. Timi Yuro's mother was a great cook and had this Italian restaurant. Everybody would eat there. If you didn't have money, she would feed you. Anyway, Phil Spector, well he had money, but starting out, he probably didn't. Nick Venet was down there a lot, too. Troy and Timi. Genius. Timi was a Number One artist in Holland before it was all over. She and Tony Williams, two of my favorite singers ever, both died in Las Vegas at separate times. Her friend was Albert Collins. I think he died there, too. He was on Imperial the same time I was. Keep in mind that Imperial and Warner Brothers were part of Liberty Records.

no reason to age

I care
to know why
you gave in
before your time
it's real sad
to be refused
but, it's no reason
to age

———

1965 started with Danny Hutton. By then, his mom had rented to me half of the red attic room, and beneath the California moon, Danny said, "It's time for you to learn about the Byrds."

We went to Melrose to a ballet studio now known as the Groundlings. And there they were, the Byrds, doing all of their first album. The place was packed with actors and factors and dream making and shaking, with heartbreaking girls standing around.

"These are our Beatles," said Danny. "This is our West Coast now."

The Beau Brummels had done it already, but these guys rocked more steady. There it was, right in front of me, and of course I didn't jump in. I was twenty-four and a half years old. I just thought it was cool. That's the kind of fool I was in 1965.

voices in my brain

last night I saw voices in my brain
of my children waiting to be born

they said "hurry, find our sweet mother"
"we're waiting to be together
the day you set you free"

yesterday I heard them cry on my telephone
"we're your future"
they said, "be brave and hang on tightly"

I can only hope that you remember
what life is going to be

to those of you
living in the future
make our present your past
be happy you're alive

Here's the Mamas and Papas story in a nutshell. The door opens. Nick Venet was expecting three people, and sees four. He compliments them all on their image. John corrects him, and says, "There's just three of us. She's the driver (points at Cass)." Nick says "Driver, do you sing?" "Yes." "Do you know the parts of each song?" "Yes." They sing for him for the first time, four part harmony. Nick is floored, tells them he'll get them on Mira Records, that they need to audition for Randy Woods and the guys who run the company. This was Black Randy Wood, former president of Vee-Jay Records, who dated one of Kim Fowley's dad's wives, Mary Fowley. No, they didn't get married. If they had gotten married, I would have had the president of Vee-Jay Records as a step-father. Oh, well. They said okay, Nick gave them a hundred and fifty dollars to see them through the weekend, and tells them where to go for the Monday meeting.

Monday morning, Barry McGuire (who was riding high on *Eve of Destruction* at the time) was called by the group to get some marijuana, as they were apprehensive and anxious about auditioning for Randy Wood and guys in suits.

So then, Barry came over, gave them the necessary refreshments to make them feel good, then called Lou Adler, because Lou had told him, "Call me if you ever hear anything good." So Barry told Lou that Mira Records was auditioning this group from New York and thought that they should jump on it, so they all barrel into Barry's car, drive to the Dunhill Records office. Lou asks them how they found Mira Records, and when the Kim Fowley/ Nick Venet elements were introduced, Lou got nervous, heard the entire story and told the group, "Don't talk to those guys any more. I'm now your producer, manager, publisher. Sign this paper, I'll give you three thousand bucks and you guys will move into your own apartment, get a car, make a record, it'll be a hit and have a wonderful life." So they sign the contract, and he walks them to the bank to cash the check, because they couldn't have cashed the check, the way they were dressed, with that sleeping bag, chicken noodle soup eating kinda soda cracker look. Nick Venet calls me 3:30 Monday afternoon and tells me, "Someone intercepted this group. They never showed up." The story's been challenged by other rock scholars, that it didn't go down this way, but this is what I remember.

Kim Fowley later dated Michelle Phillips, who I ran into at the Teen Age Fair. I had the choice of going onstage with the MC5 and jamming with them or dating Michelle Phillips and I chose her. The chance of infamy by Kim Fowley not jamming with the MC5 was because Michelle Phillips was a very attractive woman, probably still is.

Then it was time to go to England again in 1966, to meet all my 1964 friends. It was cool and it was cold. I lived on some floors and I busted some heads, didn't wake up dead, got to produce the Belfast Gypsies and Slade, when they were the N'Betweens. Slade. I met them as the N'Betweens. It was at Tiles, the club at England, where they had an All-nighter—I think they had thirteen bands on that night. It started at whatever time clubs started in England, then it went on at midnight until noon the next day. One of those dawn-to-dusk things, or nightfall to daybreak kind of shows, which were popular in England in 1966. I'd go down and everyone is on the floor, in sleeping bags. They're all sleeping. The whole audience is asleep at four or five in the morning. Here comes the N'Betweens with Noddy Holder, the great lead singer, who comes up and says, "Wake up!" with a voice that Little Richard and the Isley Brothers had. Gravel and power and poetry.

"Wake up!"

And all of them jumped up and started rocking and I said, "Aw, yes. That's rock and roll."

I jumped around and came backstage and

declared them God and I told them who Kim
Fowley was and then I said, "I demand to
produce you." And I did. Next week or so, I was in
Regent Sound and we did nine songs in one day.
That was the stuff that came out on EMI—not all
of it, but various reissues through the year. Lots
of it, but not all has come out. We did the Young
Rascals song, *You Better Run*. We did *Security* by
Otis Redding and *Hold Tight* by Davy Dee, Dozy,
Mick and Tich. We did some originals. I sang
with them on some stupid song. They didn't have
a van, and had come from Wolverton by train,
in suits and neckties and everything. The guy in
the band carried most of his drum set and there
were amps in the studios and they had their
guitars and bass. It was glorious. So we made this
record, and I went up to EMI and they released
it, and it failed. *You Better Run* was backed with
Evil Witchman. By then I was back in America
and I remember the guitar player got Kim Fowley
more than the rest of them did. Noddy Holder
had pleasant memories of me hustling the band
and recording them. Jimmy Lee tolerated me, I
think that Noddy got me partially, he went along
with it. He was just part of them. Guitar player
Dave Hill was the spirit of Slade, the way that
Joan Jett was the conscience of the Runaways,
the heartbeat of the group, the pulse of the group.
I was asked to come back. They had an EMI deal.

"Come back and work with us," they said, and
I didn't because it was 1967 and it was love-ins
and all that crap, and I never went back.

I ran into Dave Hill years later, "How've
you been?" We saw each other again when

they were Slade, when they finally were huge. Noddy mentions it in his book. I was all Sixties clothes and pre-love-in shabbiness, like a soiled Mod. When he had seen me in Germany in the seventies, I was in a three-piece suit with short, corporate hair. The guy who produced them from the Animals, Chas Chandler, and Kim Fowley and Slade all went to the Rainbow and I turned to the table and I said to Chas, "I met them too early and you met them too late." And I think I was right, because I recorded them in '66 and Chas Chandler dealt with them in the early seventies, but there were those missing years with Creem in England and Steppenwolf and Three Dog Night, and all of these things like Creedence Clearwater were going on. If Slade would've had Kim Fowley or Chas Chandler producing them at that moment, rock and roll would've been different. It was that missing time between the N'Betweens and Ambrose Slade, or maybe Ambrose Slade into the Chas Chandler chapter of Slade, where I should've been the producer. But they did well.

So, Slade spent one day in the studio with me. The Belfast Gypsies was two or three days at the most. This was a different time—you didn't spend months making records. You spent hours or days. Basically I went into a London restaurant—I can't remember the name—it was where the star musicians used to eat on Denmark Street. I walk in there and here's these moody guys from Belfast, and the McAuley brothers say, "We were in Them."

I said, "Yeah? What are you doing now?"

"We're trying to make a record."

At this very first luncheon with them, I said, "Alright, let's go down the street and make a record."

"Who are you?"

I told them who I was, and we went down to the studio and booked time and they knew I was telling the truth—I believe they did. Then we went into a pub. They had a rehearsal room above the place, and a day or two later, I brought some lyrics with me and we wrote some songs together. They had songs of their own and we had some covers, a combination of noise. Then, we went down to see Bill Farley, who was the genius who engineered and mixed for Andrew Loog Oldham era Stones, before the Dave Hassenger era at RCA and Keith Grant at Olympic. A lot of stuff was done at Regent. I think Black Sabbath was done there, I mean this guy was one of the great engineer mixers who was never given glory. He was the engineer of the Belfast Gypsies, whose name I came up with because they looked like gypsies and they were from Belfast.

The clothes that they wore on those albums, those were Kim Fowley's clothes, donated because they didn't have any interesting clothes for the album cover. They didn't wear that kind of clothes onstage or in the street, but they did on the album cover. And then they went off to Denmark after we did those records. They went away and I never saw them again. You know, you identify me with these records, but I possibly only spent one to three days with these people. Hello, goodbye. It was a singles world. We make recordings, and they become singles or they become an album or they become part of an album. I barely know the people. It's like an Emergency Room in a hospital. You don't know the people, they just come and go.

I never met the Prince or the Queen. I lived in Bayswater next to Jimi Hendrix, who one day said, "Would you like to hear my music?" It was the weekend he got in there in 1966.

Jimi Hendrix said, "Hey where you from?"

"California Sun," said Kim Fowley.

He said, "I'm from Seattle."

"Remember Gail Harris?" I asked.

"Oh yeah," said Jimi. "She had big tits, and she had a good group for the records."

And I said, "The Wailers."

He said, "Yeah, I made noise for the Spanish Castle, too."

I said, "Okay, what do you do?"

He said, "I write. I do Science Fiction Rock and Roll."

"What's that?" I said.

He said, "Look."

He opened up his sea chest that he carried all his books with him in, and he had a book by Ray Bradbury and another by Philip José Farmer.

I said, "What's this?"

He said, "This is the literature of Science Fiction Rock and Roll. Inspiration. When I read this, I make sounds with it on my guitar."

He became a star.

Hey Jimi, whats up?

battle of Hollywood

forgotten, feeling rotten
in the year of neon fun
lost in downtown Hollywood
lookin' for the sun
hazy, glaze of better days
never, ever won
I sit as cold as marble
much to sick to run

saw you down at the studio
heard the rap you gave
you claim I need your help
but I sail on a different wave
it is time to go away
to another land
to the flow of time
where someone understands

truth has got me mellow
in a magic, natural way
I've seen the dangers of the night
thought I'd never see the day
raindrops fall like angel feathers
from the cotton sky
I smile and laugh and love a lot
and hardly ever cry
if you cannot get off on that
then you live a tragic lie

I had a good time in 1966, because I had been, at that point in time, in the Mothers of Invention. I was the hype-a-phone player at Verve Records, who had the Freakout label. I knew what being crazy was all about. Keith Moon and I became friends, we hung out at various London clubs. I loaned him twenty pounds and said, "Hey Keith, I'll see you in a hundred years in Hell somewhere, or maybe never if we're lucky, but you owe me twenty English pounds." We made the rounds of all the clubs. When I'd had enough, I went back to L.A., where I was coming off the plane and going right into the L.A. riots on the Sunset Strip. Well, there I was with a sub-human jailhouse haircut and a bow-tie, watching Steven Stills lose a tooth. Peter Fonda got arrested. Crescent Heights and Sunset Strip, oh how those hippies protested.

In 1966, I was a janitor at LWG Recording Studios—L for Michael Lloyd, W for Buddy Walters and G for Jimmy Greenspoon. A lot of dirty girls came by. It was a good time to be the King of sludge. We called it The House for Homeless Groups and if you were a musician you'd get a place to sleep. If you were a musician who could play, you could drop by at night and get a free dinner. We had stew all the time. We had teenage girls making stew, cooking for us. You come in there and you could sleep on the floor in a sleeping bag, and you could have stew, served to you by sweet little sixteens—a bunch of them. You'd sleep on the floor and eat out of the can. We used to get diarrhea all the time.

And so we had Keith Moon there, we had Jim

Morrison down there, we had Keith Potger and the Seekers in there, Joey Covington, Lowell George. Imagine all of those people would show up, and it was a rehearsal room too. It was where Steppenwolf rehearsed the first album, learned *Born to Be Wild*. Mars Bonfire, composer of *Born To Be Wild,* and I became friends. He was the lead guitarist of Sparrow, which was the forerunner of Steppenwolf. Steppenwolf rehearsed *Born to Be Wild* there and that's where I learned the song, so I could do the instrumental version. Our album came out before their single came out. Of course, they had the hit, our version was just an instrumental, trying to be the West Coast Booker T. and the MG's.

The Story Of Susie. That was Bakersfield, 1960, at The Blackboard, which was the Liverpool Cavern club of Bakersfield. It's where Merle Haggard and Buck Owens developed their honky tonk style every night. And the big star of the place was Bill Woods, who was a DJ in Bakersfield, and he would go down there and do recitations, like Wink Martindale did in *Deck of Cards*, that kind of country recitation. You stand up there with a country band playing and do recitations of all kinds of country soap opera drama. Then one day, he made a record called *The Story of Susie* on Global Records. Orange label with green writing. *Alley Oop* was a big deal at the time, so they said, "Can we put Kim Fowley and Gary Paxton on as producers?"

"Sure," we said.

So they put our names on it, 'cause that was supposed to draw attention to the record.

Somehow Gary and I arranged the distribution. The record came out and got covered two times. It was going to be a big country *Welfare Cadillac* kind of hit. I took the record over to Alan Freed, who I was still in touch with because I had gone on from being his Food Runner to being the West Coast Promotion Man for Skip and Flip. Alan Freed and I had stayed in touch, because he saw me as a graduate from being food runner to the Number One record producer of *Alley Oop*.

"Good job," he said. So I brought him Bill Woods' record, *The Story of Susie*, and Alan Freed called me on the phone and said, "Let me tell you something. You are the first person to ever be involved in a White Drug Record. This is 1960, but I predict there's going to be a lot of drug music out, because that's what's happening in the culture. Others are going to make music to do with drugs."

So Alan Freed totally predicted the Psychedelic Era. He was six or seven years early, but he was right—*Susie* became the template for Elliott Ingber and *Don't Bogart That Joint*. Elliott formed the Fraternity of Man after the Mothers of Invention and ended up with Captain Beefheart, but before that he was in Phil (Spector) Harvey's band doing *Bumbershoot*, and then after that he was in the Gamblers. *Moondawg*, produced by Nick Venet. The Gamblers of course did *Teen Machine* for Last Chance Records, owned by Kim Fowley. Elliot came over to The House For Homeless Groups, where I lived, and he brought over all the guys from Fraternity of Man. Richie Hayward was on drums, who would later go on to be in that group with Lowell George, pre-Little Feat Richie Hayward. In Fraternity of Man, I was the Pig Pen of the group. Remember when the Grateful Dead would have Jerry Garcia as one lead singer and then Pig Pen would come in and rip the crowd up. When the Fraternity of Man played on certain days, their singer, Lawrence "Stash" Wagner, wasn't that good at whipping the crowd up. I was, and I'd come in there in a Pig Pen position and I would get things going with the crowd. Kim Fowley is great onstage for getting a crowd to be loud and vulgar, and scream and yell. I'm the Ultimate Party Front Man. So those guys used to come over and worship, as a religious artifact, Bill Woods doing *The Story of Susie* and the B-side *Gossip*. They based their whole sound on that record and wrote their own songs, but that was the mood they used. That was the inspiration. And their record *Don't Bogart Me*, which we used to call *Don't Bogart That Joint*, that became a song in the *Easy Rider* soundtrack, which became The First Rock and Roll Movie Soundtrack that ever existed. Later, I did *American Graffiti*, which was the second movie that did significant business with a rock and roll soundtrack—ten million copies sold. Kim Fowley produced two songs on the album, *At The Hop* and *She's So Fine*.

Frank Zappa was very gifted, but he maybe wasn't as great as they said he was. Overrated. Just like those guys Nick Cave, Elvis Costello, Nick Drake, Frank Zappa. They all seem to be given Parthenon, Jesus Christ, Buddha worship. They were good, or they are good, but it wasn't *that* good. It was pretty good and there were great moments. Everybody has some great moments and some awful moments and boring moments, or no moments, and Frank was very good at what he did. We all know what he did. And his widow is a genius for keeping it going, and the kids are good at what they do, it's all complimentary, but...

Who are the best guys and girls? I've named them before: John Lennon, Jim Morrison, Jerry Lee Lewis, and Etta James and Sandi Shaw and Dusty Springfield. Mary Weiss had great moments, but God, those records, wow! Phil Spector, his work: sensational. Joe Meek, George Martin, those are the obvious. Roy Orbison is God. When he opens his mouth and sings, it's like the guy in the Ink Spots, just like the guy in the Skyliners, Jimmy Beaumont. I mean, whoa! They changed lives when they opened their mouths and sang! Duane Eddy—well, that was often Al Casey on guitar, he was probably the brain of Lee Hazlewood. Jody Reynolds for that one song, *Endless Sleep*. Thomas Wayne, and those one hit wonders and all those guys. I mean, possibly Frank Zappa's greatest moment was on *Freak Out*, and then after a while, it was music for him and his fans went with him to all kinds of places. But he was alright, he gave me a shot. Thank you, Frank. Too bad I didn't stay, but that's okay. It was fun. Kim Fowley sang *Help I'm A Rock* on *Freakout*, the unreleased live album, and on some unreleased outtakes. Zappa called me his Brian Jones.

Well, I was called the Napoleon imitator, and that was in 1966 too. That's old news. I covered

They're Coming To Take Me Away by Napoleon XIV as Kim Fowley on CBS Records UK, and I charted in New Zealand and Denmark. The Napoleon XIV record did not. His record charted everywhere else.

1967

365 days went by
where was I?
pergatory
Hell
or Heaven

don't know
don't remember
nothin'

what happened?
not much
'cause I've lost touch
with 1967

no memory
no memory lane
no pain
no tears
no regrets
oh I can't forget what happened
God only knows

1967 is this: I did Love-Ins. It was fun, I didn't consider it work. That's why I didn't know where my work was. I would go to Elysian Park or Griffith Park on Sundays. John Carpenter from the Ken Kesey world (i.e. Merry Pranksters) was the stage manager and we started at six in the morning when all the people on acid would come by and do "oom," and they'd have their incense sticks and then Dennis Wilson would always show up. He wasn't on acid, but he just enjoyed it and he would play bongos and congas. He was kind of like a Max Weinberg, only leading everybody chanting "oom." And then people like the Peanut Butter Conspiracy always seemed to be the first band on—they liked to play early. They'd come on after "oom," and it was quite interesting.

As the nights wore on, it would go from six in the morning to two in the morning. Sometimes twenty thousand people would show up. There was always a makeshift stage. Girls would take their tops off and myself and other musicians would crawl under the stage and have sex with them. So that was our Motel Room on a Love-In basis. Sometimes there were twenty or thirty bands. Sometimes bands would get stuck in traffic and then you'd have to make a makeshift band with whoever was standing around.

We had lost babies and lost dogs we'd hold up and say, "Who does this baby belong to?" or "Who does this dog belong to?"

Sometimes the dogs and the babies were claimed, other times they weren't. Hoyt Axton would come out, who was a famous songwriter who wrote *Joy to the World* and *The Pusher* by

Steppenwolf, among others. His mother co-wrote *Heartbreak Hotel* with Elvis Presley. But anyway, he'd get up there, take his shirt off and start jumping around. Chris Darrow was there with the Kaleidoscope—Jimmy Page's favorite instrumental band ever—and they would play. Steve Miller made his first appearance when Chet Helms brought him in and said,

"Here he is, everybody. Stand back."

And he was good. And then it got dark and around 2 in the morning, I'd ask everybody to pick up trash and clean the park, and they would. There was never any trash there. There weren't any riots or anything. Out of that evolved the album *Love Is Alive and Well*, which was on Tower Records. It was a document of what went on from my point of view at the Love-Ins. And that's all she wrote.

Kim wasn't a drug person. I'd had polio in '46 and in '57—one was Paralytic and the second was Non-Paralytic—plus I had Pneumonia nine times in and out of '46 to '59. So when you're a sickly, you aren't getting high and drunk, because that's for all the guys on the football team from high school—growing up and thinking they're immortal. They're the one who O.D. The guys whose childhood is interwoven, intermingled with hospitals—we don't get high because we're medicated, sometimes against our will. Childhood trauma and medication in a hospital setting, means we don't get high. Nobody needs the problem.

I recorded the Soft Machine in England in 1966—Kevin Ayers, Daevid Allen (later of Gong), Robert Wyatt and Mike Ratledge. I went to see the them and Pink Floyd at the Roundhouse in Chalk Farm with Mark Wirtz Peters, yes, that was his name back then. I know his real name is Mark Peter Wirtz, but he was Mark Peters back then. He produced *Grocer Jack* later. It was called *Excerpt From A Teenage Opera*, which was *Grocer Jack* performed by Keith West of Tomorrow. Mark produced that record and it went to Number One everywhere in the world, except America and Japan. So here they were. Pink Floyd with a young and dashing Syd Barrett. The other group was the Soft Machine. They were a four piece and Mark said, "Which one do I produce?"

I said, "The ones who don't know my name. Whoever yells my name out will be who I produce." So we walk in and Robert Wyatt yells out, "Kim Fowley! Mothers of Invention! *Freakout!*"

And I turned to Mark and said, "You get Pink Floyd." So Mark got Pink Floyd and he took them over to EMI where he had a producing arrangement and they signed the band. Then they wouldn't let him produce them, because at that point he hadn't done the *Excerpt From A Teenage Opera* album yet, so Norman Smith— one of the Beatles engineers who had his own hit records later as a singer—got it. I cut *Love Makes Sweet Music* and *Reelin' Feelin' and Squeelin'* with the Soft Machine. Only *Reelin'* made it to their first 45, as the b-side. They recut *Love Makes Sweet Music* with Chas Chandler. People tell me *Reelin'* also came out as *Shadows In The Sun* by some group called Beautiful. That came out on some weird label and there's an instrumental on the back, which is actually pretty good. But that wasn't the Soft Machine, it was some guys from the House For Homeless Groups, and that label came out of the House For Homeless Groups. I stayed friends with Robert Wyatt and Kevin Ayers. I never saw the other guys again. One day, I ran into Robert Wyatt in Hollywood.

He said, "Jimi Hendrix just recorded *Fluffy Turkeys*," which was a 1969 Kim Fowley song. Jimi Hendrix was supposed to be producing that group Eire Apparent that was on Buddha, from somewhere in New York, maybe Long Island. And he's down there at Robert's visiting, because Eire Apparent also played on one of his tours with Soft Machine. And they never showed up. Jimi had studio time, so he said, "Robert, what do we do? We're sitting here and the band hasn't shown up."

Robert said, "Let me play you Kim Fowley's new record *Fluffy Turkeys* on Original Sound." The label copy said the name of the artist was "The Incredible Kim Fowley."

Jimi Hendrix said, "I want to cover that right now. You play drums and I'll play guitar and bass."

So he covered that song, and somewhere there is a tape—it's probably unmarked—which is *Fluffy Turkey* by Jimi Hendrix—guitar, bass and voice—and Robert Wyatt. In Wyatt's book, it mentions that it was done in England. No, it was done at the same TTG studio, the same one Tom Wilson produced The Mothers of Invention with Frank Zappa and Kim Fowley singing.

> *drugs remind*
> *the lord of garbage*

of the empty parents
who relied on bad dreams
drugs to get them high
I just slide across the soundstage of
the victims that can't cry

Cathy Richards' *Wild Thing* was recorded after Nancy Sinatra had done *These Boots Are Made For Walking* and it had gone to Number One, so folks at World Pacific thought that Cathy, Buddy Rich's daughter, should do a record. I was hired to produce her. We did *Wild Thing* backed with *Paper Tiger*. During my time at World Pacific, I also produced Elfstone doing *Louisiana Teardrops,* and *Beat the Clock. Beat the Clock* was a Toys cover and that's on Crown Records. Well, anyway, I go in the studio and Michael Lloyd was involved in that and some of St. John Green played on it, and maybe the drummer of Bread. And we did it in three hours. "My name is Cathy…. and I'm WILD." Remember that moment? I think she was thirteen years old. I talked to her later about those days. Now she's in her forties of fifties. She has fond memories of it. Buddy Rich wasn't very happy that his thirteen-year-old daughter was saying, "My name is Cathy and I'm wild." He yelled at the guys at World Pacific, who he was under contract to, "Why did you let that weird guy produce my daughter doing that?" Because Nancy can say, "My boots are made for walking," but Cathy can't say, "My name is Cathy and I'm wild." Buddy was a karate expert and he indicated that he might come down and "sort me out." Bring it on! It never happened and the record floats around. It's one of those records that people find ... and cherish.

> ***not jealous or afraid***
> ***ode to a one nite stand***
>
> *in a sweet embrace*
> *I hesitated*
> *you encouraged me*
> *to set you free*
>
> *I'm not jealous*
> *or afraid*
> *to be happy*
> *but not betrayed*
> *someday we'll love each other*
> *but maybe not today*

—•—

1968 was great. Kim Fowley pretended to be his own twin on the cover of *Outrageous*. I was born to win. It was time for me to do an album. I did it in four hours and it was called *Outrageous* and Ed Caraeff photographed me like I had a twin brother. On an Elvis Aaron and Jesse Garron level. When you see the album cover, you think there are two guys, but I don't have a twin brother.

Ed Caraeff took the picture. The famous eighteen year-old boy wonder from the land of blood and thunder—Southern California. Ed impressed with a picture of Jimi Hendrix setting his guitar on fire. Oh yeah. Rodney Bingenheimer and Kim Fowley used to take Ed Caraeff around to all the Sunset Strip record companies. It went down just like this: Ed would take a picture he mounted ten by twelve onto a cardboard and we'd march into the office and say, "Here's a gift." They hired him on the spot, thought he was hot—the future photographer to break into rock and roll. Take a picture of your favorite band, make them understand that you can capture them in black and white or color too. Mount a picture and you can hand it over to the manager and they will hire you.

The *Outrageous* band was Fast Eddie Hoh, the drummer who was on super sessions with Mike Bloomfield and Stephen Stills. He allegedly went into a Mental Hospital after we did the record. I don't know if that's true or not. Then one of the keyboard players might've fallen in front of a train or jumped in front of a train in England. And then the rest of the crew, except for Mars Bonfire and I, could've been on acid—we're not sure about that. But we had Three Dog Night bass player Joe, the guitar player Mike (also of Three Dog Night), Jimmy Greenberg on organ, and Joe Sherman on bass. On rock and roll steel guitar, Red Rhodes, later of the Fraternity of Man.

Mars Bonfire was the music director. I produced it, I sang it—it was all improv, and the album came out and charted Billboard (#198). It got me a fan letter from Ted Nugent and an offer to perform in Detroit by Mike Quattro, which I did not accept because the deal wasn't right.

Allegedly, the Attorney General of Florida or somebody in the Attorney General's office in Tallahassee, was driving to work and heard

a lyric in *Animal Man*, "I want to kill you,"
and there was some law at the time in Florida
that you cannot threaten anyone's life on the
airwaves. There was gonna be some thing about
bringing Kim Fowley in leg irons and handcuffs
to Florida to await his trial, for threatening the
listenership with, "I want to kill you." The law
enforcement from Florida called up Liberty
Records, which distributed Imperial—it was one
of their affiliated labels—about where I was, but
they also thought it might be a bunch of college
DJ's pretending to be the Attorney General's
office, which would have put me ahead of Jim
Morrison. Wasn't he arrested down there for
indecency in '69?

Okay, so Kim was banned. But we don't even
know if that was a phone call hoax. That was a
milestone for me as an artist, because the world
had only heard *The Trip*, which was banned in
'65. And then here's something that was under
scrutiny for being horrific.

Then in '68, I had to do a second album and
they said, "You can't do any wild stuff anymore."
So I had to do the comedy album *Good Clean Fun*,
on which the world got to hear Warren Zevon. He
wrote some songs on there, he played guitar and
keyboard. And the Bonzo Dog Band were also on
there, uncredited. Vivian Stanshall also showed
up with Neil Innes, later to be in Monty Python.
They're on there. That album came out and Rex
Reed, a famous critic from New York City, thought
it was genius, said so in Newsweek, and that was
it. The rock audience said, "Wait a minute. Is
that it? We want more noise like *Outrageous*,"

but it wasn't permitted by the record company, Imperial Records.

Somewhere in '68, I recorded the album I just mentioned, *Born to Be Wild*, the second album was *Outrageous*, and then of course the Rex Reed approved, but not selling, album Good Clean Fun. Richard and Thomas Frost were on there, they had a chart single. They sang as the background group. Rodney Bingenheimer also sang on the record, *Searching For A Teenage Queen*. And Harlowe from Sylvester, the Harlots—but not the New York Harlots—the San Francisco Harlots—and on the album, too.

Gene Vincent showed up sometime in '69 to be produced by me. More about Gene and Kim Fowley a few pages from now. Here's a poem about the shallow Silver Sixties Kim Fowley, the troubled me. This appeared in lieu of liner notes on the back cover of the 1968 *Born to Be Wild* instrumental album.

the world owes you a living

I am a mind of a monster
in the body of a boy.
I, the heavy evil
highway bandit
prowl by car and
prowl by midnight feet
I say it in your sisters'
faces, whip so wicked
rope so tight
my fingers rip through

silk and perfume,
body paint the bedspread
bright.
I crave warm fluffy things
kittens, hamsters,
feathered fish, crouching
in the country heat,
eating legs of chicken hawks
the barnyard grease dribbles
down my chin as I make
an important space discovery
while feasting
my human body holds me
its lifetime prisoner.
I escape through the tongues
splashing into smiles, tears,
yells and screams.
it is hard for me to appear
when the world wants me to
on the surface of my human body.
materialistically, the world
expects me to communicate
on its own terms.
I look back and see none.
reality brings about a change.
straight people are crazy.
by being born wild into
this universe
you are hereby endowed
by nature with all you need

for life, liberty
and the pursuit of happiness.
the world owes you a living.
flaming creatures
go wild until you get it.

———

Sky Saxon…oh God, okay. Richie Marsh had a peculiar voice. He became Sky Saxon later. He sang like an Elf and a Hamster and Mick Jagger, all at the same time. And he had a band and they had a sound and he had a Squeaky Voice and he was quite an individual, and he had Charisma. It was a Helium kind of hamster-elf-Jagger phrasing thing and those records are interesting to listen to as long as he was on GNP Crescendo with myself producing *Falling Off the Edge of My Mind*, *Wild Blood*, and the lost classic, *Shock Waves*. Then Jimmie Maddin produced the first hit, whatever that was called. Maybe it wasn't a hit nationally—but it was the first L.A. hit—and Sky produced everything else. For that moment of time, he was amazing, but the label unfortunately didn't have the distribution and the sales, because if he'd had a bigger label behind him, this stuff would've done better. But then, maybe a big label wouldn't have given him the chance that Gene Norman gave him. He's the genius guy who ran GNP Crescendo.

I didn't know Sky that well, other than hello. We never ate dinner together or lunch. He was a guy I'd say "hi" to from '59 to '66.

"Hello, what's up? I heard your record," or whatever. He was trying for years to get a deal and then he finally got lucky with the Seeds records on GNP Crescendo, and that was it. I remember meeting him and I played him the guitar and voice demo of *Falling Off the Edge of My Mind* and *Wild Blood*, which Mars Bonfire played on, with me singing. *Shock Waves*, we just went in. Sky learned the songs from my demos. And we did it. And then his manager Archie Sullivan, who was the same guy who put out *Teenage Queen*, or tried to put out *Teenage Queen*, and *Baby Hip* by the Village Colors on his own record label and didn't even have the money for the labels. They made the test pressing and it stopped there.

Well, Archie Sullivan was a great guy. He was in the restaurant business or something and he was very sincere and he convinced Sky, or Sky convinced him, and suddenly the Seeds ended up on MGM. And that was the beginning of the end because the Seeds didn't have records and Sky Saxon didn't make any records that made sense. He made records that are always under different names and different combinations of people and all those experiments and all the travelling and all the whatever he went through. I didn't know him then.

The last time I saw Sky Saxon, he had on a pair of brass knuckles and he came up behind me and slugged me in the back of the head and I fell on the ground. The cops stopped him—and this was in Las Vegas. The cops said, "If you want to press charges, we will arrest him. But you'll have to come back and go to court and hire lawyers. If you don't want to do that, we won't arrest him. Because if you're not going to press charges, why waste time and money?"

And I said, "You're right," because I knew the guy didn't have any money. And so he got me from behind, good for him. I outlived him so far, that's my revenge.

if I died today who would say goodbye a/k/a message to myself

you got no wind chimes/no lanterns
no beauty
no love
just ugly and fear
your man made world
it's a psycho ward
you're not respected
just disliked and ignored
you're building monuments
to dead end dreams
tears fall/the needle drops
then it's the beatings and the screams
the games that hunt you
got more guns
then the police
faceless
graceless
what's your release?
endless blue skies saw you crying
in the sunshine

at ground zero
no body cares
lower than low
life isn't fair

it means
nothin' to you
you're not even there
alone in your room
playing blue solitaire

if you died today?
who would say goodbye
a thief goin through your pockets
or a lady tellin' lies?

Saturday night
you ain't been paid
life runs bye
nobodys home
you ain't painting the town
nobodys there
nobody shares
the lives of un-touchable clowns

you're like an unwanted child
waitin' for a car
to take you
to heaven
you got nothin'
left to give
no reason to live
in the safety of your pain
you can't stop the rain

you're nowhere
a whispering stone
in your small empty room

you're always alone
a forgotten soul
barely alive
still In denial
but you gotta survive

⸺·⸺

Oh, well. Genius, isn't that? Turning thirty, I think. When you turn thirty, you think it's all over, because in America, you graduate high school when you're seventeen or eighteen. Then you get out of college at twenty-one or twenty-two, and then you have your apprenticeship from twenty-four to twenty-five. Then you're supposed to make a fortune and start a family and marry a girl for the rest of your life, and if none of that is done by the time you're thirty, you're statistically a piece of shit. So I bought into that for a second, and felt that maybe it was over. Little did I know that I had forty-three more years to go, because I'm seventy-three now.

If I died today, who would say goodbye? My answer is: my estate, my attorneys and accountants. But at that time, I hadn't made a deal with death. Now, I'm sort of at the level of, "Well, I'm not going to wake up as Brad Pitt in the morning, or Jake Gyllenhaal. I'm not going to be somebody who an eighteen-year-old girl is going to masturbate to with all her pink-feathered dildos, with all my naked photos in her bedroom. Nope. I missed that boat, so I get to be the Timothy Leary version of Clint Eastwood if I'm lucky. Clint Eastwood is my hero. That guy is making quality work in film and he's eighty-three years old. Good composer, too. He just carries on, which is what you're supposed to do. You know how it is, *American Idol*, you can only be a certain age to compete, and if you're a model, it's eleven to twenty-three. Getting a record deal, they prefer you to be under twenty-five.

So when you're an old person, and you can be an "old person" at ten, but you do wonder, because when you're dead, no one cares. They're glad you're gone, then about three to five years after you're dead, they start reviewing your work and then decide that "Kim Fowley was actually rather gifted." But I'm kind of hard to deal with as a human, because they can't swallow it, the Kim Fowley thing sticks in your throat and you choke on it, or you puke and get sick as it leaves your system.

In 1969 I was getting ready to do Live Peace in Toronto, just finishing Gene Vincent's album *I'm Back and I'm Proud*. He wrote and sang about death. Good lord, he was a gloomy guy. Nice person, but he had his moments of pathos.

1969

1969
was like cool
mountain lion
gasoline mixed in
It was the end
of the sixties
no more
Woodstock
no more

Charles Manson
no more
surfing girls
no more hot rods
the gods had
disappeared
and gone away
and 1970
was about to start
With all the
broken dreams
and all the
broken hearts
we stood there
silver sixties
slid away into
the gray of yesterday

1969—it was time for Gene Vincent to be produced by Kim Fowley. He showed up and he was on his way out of living. He carried a gun in his boot and he had his wife Jackie with him, his wife at the time, who was Mickie Most's sister-in-law from South Africa, and Gene was a mercenary in South Africa. Well, according to him. Now was he? Who knew, Gene thought he was, meaning he did fighting for various armies down there. There were all these political skirmishes going on.

It was a country-approached album. He gave us the versions of some of the older songs and Jimmy Page called up to be on the session and Gene said "no" to him. He wanted Johnny Meeks from the Blue Caps. Meeks showed up and they argued, so it wasn't astounding. Skip Battin on bass, Red Rhodes, Greg Johnson on piano, Mars Bonfire on rhythm. I cannot remember who the drummer was. I was disappointed in the record and so was Gene, because we wanted to go to Mississippi and record in the Malaco Studio. Malaco, which became a big deal R&B label later, was just opening and it had a tremendous sound in there and it was by water. So Gene could've gone fishing with the musicians and the Malaco studio band, which he liked to do, and then go in the studio and do Southern rock and roll.

It would've been like when he was produced in Nashville, by Ken Nelson. If you put Gene in the South, then he's Gene Vincent. Gene Vincent in England or Gene Vincent recording here in Hollywood, not quite the same. Since he was from Virginia, he had an affinity for his homeland of Dixie, you know? And they wouldn't let us. And we fought and fought over that and they won. Shame on you, David Anderle. You should have let it happen.

Who are "they"? Elektra, who was distributing John Peel's record label Dandelion in the US. Clive Selwood, he didn't like me. He didn't understand Gene. They wanted a version of the Ken Nelson record produced in '57 in Nashville. I said, "Well, then let me go to Mississippi with him. You can't get grease out of Hollywood." At least not in those days. So we had to record in the artsy fartsy studios of Elektra where they had incense and peppermint kind of décor. There were Persian throw rugs in there and psychedelic sketches. Not conducive to gut-bucket-rockabilly/redneck-country-driving rock and roll.

People like John Sebastian would walk in with his Laurel Canyon twelve hundred dollar dog. And one day Paul Rothschild—the Doors' producer—and one of the Doors walked up with two hot blondes, surf beasts, uninvited. And Gene was about to do *Sexy Ways*, the Hank Ballard and the Midnighters song.

He said, "Who is that producer and those people who just entered my studio uninvited?"

I said, "Paul Rothschild, a guy from the Doors, and two blonde surf beasts." At the time, Linda Ronstadt was in the room because she had called me and said, "Can I volunteer to be Food Runner? I wanna study under Gene Vincent and see how he approaches singing." So Gene looks at Paul Rothschild and the Doors guy—it might've been the drummer, I'm not sure who it was—with the two girls, and said, "Hey, Linda Ronstadt is more rock and roll than the producer of the Doors or the Doors member. I've got a boot with a gun, I'm gonna pull out the gun. I'm a dead shot and you will all die when I start firing at you. Leave my studio." They took off.

And then Gene sang a great vocal. It's the best vocal on the album, *I'm Back and I'm Proud*. He put the gun back in his shoe and sang. That was a great rock and roll moment. Rodney Bingenheimer was there. Linda Ronstadt was beaming, "I'm more rock and roll than the Doors, yeah!" And she never made a rock and roll record better than the Doors, but at that moment she was more rock and roll than the Doors.

Gene Vincent had this leg problem, which has

been well documented, and I had my leg problem with polio and my hand problems with polio, and we bonded as two cripples. He was more of an obvious cripple than I was, but I was nevertheless damaged from when I had polio, and secondly, we were both emotionally crippled. So we were devastated human beings. He was a very nice person who was very considerate.

Gene was the biggest influence on John Lennon of anybody. Of all of the people who might have influenced John Lennon, the persona of Gene singing those songs and how he staged them gave him his Rock and Roll identity, or a part of the basis of his process to be a Beatle, to be John Lennon the performer or writer, the guy who conjured up moods and whatnot. And he also inspired Paul McCartney. I think in later performances, Paul McCartney did some Gene Vincent music.

He was the first guy to ever wear Black Leather on an International Scale in a Rock and Roll Context, and we all know that Black Leather means in Rock and Roll. I'm too exhausted in a possible deathbed here to rattle on about what Leather means to Rock and Roll. I'm sure we all know what it means, it means Strength, Darkness, Sex. It means Power. It means Mystery. It means everything, and Gene was the First White Man in Leather. He told me a story that somewhere in Minnesota, a Gene Vincent imitator dressed in Gene Vincent-type leather shot and killed somebody in a liquor store and the police arrested Gene for the murder. He said, "Nope, it's not me. I was onstage and I have several thousand witnesses at the same time that my imitator killed this person." And sure enough, it was the imitator that pulled the trigger, not Gene. He was dressed up like Gene and robbed the liquor store and the guy died behind the counter. So Gene was the first Rock and Roll guy in Leather to be arrested for Murder too. That's pretty cool. That was the story he told. I don't know what town it was, but it was somewhere in Minnesota back in the Blue Caps days.

He was a very gentle soul, but very needy at the same time. He needed friends and he needed support and he needed relief and he had this tremendous pain that he had to co-exist with every day because of his leg problems. I'm not sure what they were caused by or what they were, but amputation was constantly suggested to him and he constantly rejected it. And so at the moment in this book, I'm in a post-cancer, surgical recall, pain and medication state, and I know how hard it is to have all of this horrifying pain and you're supposed to make rational statements about it—whatever your reality is— for people who aren't in pain and somehow try to recreate it and somehow try to communicate in a rational way, and everybody around you is appalled because it's really awful to listen or watch it happen. Until you read it or you hear it. And then you jack off, and you smoke a joint and you pass the beer around and say, "Read this, listen to that, look at this!" And out of all this horror and pain of people who are crippled and never get well, God! We're competing with all you able-bodied people and you guys are sloppy.

You're sloppy about eating sugar and all the things you do to destroy your life. The rest of us are just trying to catch a breath so we can make the next mistake. Gene had seven producers. I was the only disabled one.

In '69, I met, through Tom Ayers, the Sir Douglas Quintet. Tom Ayers was the producer of *Hot Pastrami* by the Dartells. When he asked me to produce the next Gene Vincent album, by then he had gone up to Buddha, so he didn't have a deal. He left Dandelion and I introduced him, Gene Vincent, to Tom Ayers, and Tom Ayers produced him in '70. But before that—in the last part of '69—I co-wrote *Michoacan* with Atwood Allen, the Electric Ice Man from San Antonio, who allegedly made the best-blended marijuana recipes in the United States. He would take elements of some other herbs from the Mexican American border and whip it up, and apparently it gave you quite a jolt. But even though I do Drug Records like *The Trip* and *Let's Get Blasted*, I haven't smoked that stuff since I found out I have a tobacco allergy, number one. And number two, why do I need to be high? I'm already Insane/ Crazy/Enlightened. So Doug Sahm, Augie and the rest of them learned *Michoacan* and then it found its way into Kris Kristofferson's first movie called *Cisco Pike*. Although the original title *The Dealer*, that was better. And then he covered the song on his only live album that ever charted on Columbia. That was interesting and I was happy about that.

And then we see the end of the year. We have Kim Fowley with John Lennon and Yoko Ono,

Eric Clapton, members of Plastic Ono band, also Klaus Voormann on bass, and Alan White on drums—he later became the drummer of Yes—at Live Peace: The Rock and Roll Revival, Toronto, 1969. There's been a tremendous amount written about that, the Rock and Roll Revival. Bo Diddley, Jerry Lee Lewis, Little Richard, blah blah blah, all were up there and the Doors closed the show. Nobody photographed Jim Morrison and John Lennon together. It would have been a Great T-shirt today to wear. And the opening act—are you ready for this? Screaming Lord Sutch. What a night. The best act? Tony Joe White fronting Booker T. and the MG's. That night, Tony Joe White was Elvis. Sun Records Elvis. And that night, Booker T. and the MG's were Creedence Clearwater backing Elvis, I mean only it was this giant stadium sound. I mean wow, what a moment. Kim Fowley—purple suit, white shoes, and a chartreuse green shirt—doing what I did at the Love-Ins, from 6:00 AM- 2AM. It was John Lennon's first show after leaving the Beatles, and the Silver Sixties ended forever.

what are the colors of the wind?

lost souls gathered in the pouring rain
mysteries of the wind at the crossroads
men without a star can't run forever
cool blue leather saints forever mystified

what are the colors of the wind?
the view from the edge of paradise

is one of smoke and tin
what are the colors of the wind?
in the land of a thousand lakes
clean air is growing thin

lost forever what they needed
wheels of fortune lose contact with the everyday
dancing above the hills
silver rivers are frozen shadows
the gold coast is turning grey

beneath the laughter
are lands of silence
voices in the blue room
there's more to do than fall asleep

lost cities of the world eternal fandango
victories of art and science
human factors of formation
kings of oblivion
can't take away the tears
sweet dreams give no dream vacation

———•———

Well this is my version of what happened to
me. I don't know if really happened or not, but
I think it did. I'm holding back a lot of stuff
because it's overwhelming in its darkness and it
would be a sad read. This is a book of poetry, and
I'm merely showing the audience, or readership,
what it was like to be a part of show business in
Hollywood, and out of this crappy upbringing,
what was created. I know that ever since I've had

withered atrophy arms and legs and body parts. Not every girl liked to see Kim Fowley naked because of it. In the world of Troy Donahue taking his shirt off, nobody wanted to see polio arms in the silver sixties or nifty fifties or the sporty forties, although in the world of junkies, I'm bedroom body ready for seduction.

> *green trees*
> *rescue me*
> *blue, blue skies*
> *find eyes and ears*
> *for these words*
> *someday my audience will surely be*
> *my fans and family.*

It wasn't a diary as much as an SOS or missiles being launched from this Skeleton Giraffe. As I grow older, I see a pattern, and for those of you who are jacking off or smoking dope, banging your head, and cutting your wrists to this shit, it was totally isolation—me on my own all the way up from 1939 to '57. I learned how to talk. I learned how to lead a gang. I learned how to not be paralyzed.

Then by '59, I was out there. I wasn't an actor like my parents, but I became an actor in life. I used theatrical illusion to reinvent myself for whoever I was trying to get something from, whether it be an audience, a band, or a song. Or a guy in an office to buy something so that the audience could find out about it. So, one day, you find yourself with twenty-eight personalities that you can pull out of a hat in short exposures. But in terms of having any relationship with any human: none. There's no wiring here that supports intimacy or trust. And yes, in war you have guys who you are fighting, you have a common enemy with, and I have friends when we're battling in a band to get heard by the public or we're trying to get a record company or studio to buy something. We're all friends because we all have the same goal, but once that project or the gig is over, I never see these people again and they never see me.

I find a new set of people to interact with. And then, every now and then, some girl or woman will show up and say, "My God, you're so fascinating." And it's the Kim Fowley product that's fascinating. It's the Seduction of Checkbooks, or getting the media to co-operate. That's what turns them on. But then when they apply it to their own orgasm or their own "Pass the peas" at their parents' house for dinner, suddenly I'm Rasputin or I'm The Hunchback of Notre Dame or I'm covered in sores and they start screaming and running.

> *wounded in these wars*
> *the lord of garbage*
> *swallows hard and drinks*
> *slowly*
> *softly*
> *the medicine called compromise*

> *compromise*
> *is worse than the battles*
> *that have been*
> *lost*

If you're remarkable, you'd better have balls. You wear them on your chest if you're a woman, and you wear them underneath your penis if you're a man, because if you're wonderful in any way, somebody will fuck with you. Just like if you're horrible in any way, they're gonna fuck with you. The world is for the average and the common. Those are the people who never hurt— they just fall asleep. The rest of us, we're the Walking Wounded. I outlived Sky Saxon and he thought he was smarter than me.

In other words, if I would've died with Big Bopper, Buddy Holly and Richie Valens in 1959, or OD'd in 1969 and left this book behind, you'd be in hell and heaven over this. Except I got to Hollywood the day they died. What I'm trying to get you to understand is that I had a rock and roll life even though the rock and roll stopped. I am still out here on a wire. I am still out here on the edge of my mind falling, with fits of sanity. Going through all this weird, horrible stuff and cranking out magic. This is the back-story of how it is and was, and these rock and roll statements were lived all the time. I'm just giving you anecdotes.

You can say, "Well here's the poems and prose from that time, and this is what the guy was going through." So you have the poems taking it one place, and the prose is explaining under what conditions this crap was created. It gives a different insight. We've all heard Bach and Beethoven. We've all heard Little Richard, but what were they going through when they wrote these songs? What was going on that caused that to happen? And I think that for every person who wants to read a poem or lyric, the fact that all these words are the back-story that was going on simultaneously, makes for a page-turner. What's going to happen the next year? Does the guy go crazy?

Imagine what it must have been like being Gene Vincent and all those guys who had to live through this shit too. I mean other guys from the Fifties and Sixties had to stumble through the fucking seventies, eighties and nineties. What was that journey like? It's possibly an ugly story. The kid stuff makes you cry, because it is sad. But it happened and I did write poetry and lyrics during that time and I kept going so I could end up at this moment as your writer.

I've never had a book about me of any kind. There are people who've said, "Oh, you should write a book someday." And I always told them, "It won't be the book you want me to write," because everybody who wants you to write a book, who is a literary manager or an editor or a publisher. They always want a book on the part of your life that they'd like the best or that they would want to promote or they would know how to sell.

I know this is your least favorite part, but unfortunately I didn't OD and I didn't die at the time and I had to suffer thirty years of this shit. I mean, it was hard enough living through this, and I should celebrate some of this if I can, but it's awfully hard. My career lasted beyond 1969. And if I lived like a human being I wouldn't be able to do this, so the whole way, and I mean not just 1939 to '69, I mean today, it's awful 'cause I don't even have heat where I live. If I had lived better then I wouldn't be able to do all the recordings I do or the movies I do. And so I get to be John Waters and Sam Phillips at the same time. I don't mind being the Outlaw King of America.

> I am better than Elvis.
> I am better than JFK.
> I am better than the Beatles.
> BECAUSE I EXIST!

Epilogue

DID YOU CRY, throw up, smile or begin slowly to die? Probably. One of those horrible things moved you to get this far through the painful pages of my rumble ravings. The next two volumes will finish me off. You'll have the whole gory story by then. Tell all your friends. They can read all this truth, too. Then you cats and kittens can speculate how much of this junk is true.

Answer: all of it. All of it that's fit to print, that is.

I bled for you to get this down. I wanted you to know I was here on planet earth. Trying to find a woman, lover and a friend. Thank you for being my new friend. You've ridden shotgun with me through the broken mirrors of yesterday and today. There's no tomorrow for Kim Fowley. Only trouble. Stay tuned for the next two books. They will change your life. Pray for me tonight. I'm out there, somewhere in the dark looking for a place to hide. This book is dedicated to the bride of Frankenstein. It is a shame that I never found you.

Be happy if you can. Thanks for your time.

> Sincerely,
> Kim Fowley
> Somewhere In The Shadows

WATCH FOR THE
NEXT VOLUME OF
LORD OF
GARBAGE